FINGER ALPHABET COOL KIDS

36 WORD SEARCH PUZZLES

with the

AMERICAN SIGN LANGUAGE ALPHABET

ADVERBS

LEGENDARYMEDIA
PUBLISHING

First published in 2014 by LegendaryMedia Publishing
Windmuehlstrasse 4, 60329 Frankfurt am Main, Germany

Copyright © 2014 LegendaryMedia, www.legendarymedia.de
Copyright illustrations & hand shape drawings © Lassal, www.lassal.de

All rights reserved. No part of this publication may be reproduced, stored in a retrieval system, or transmitted, in any form or by any means, electronic, mechanical, photocopying, recording or otherwise, without prior written permission by the copyright holder. Any person or persons who do any unauthorised act in relation ot this publication may be liable to criminal persecution and civil claims for damages.

ISBN: 978-3-86469-108-9
LM003-002US-ADV-E1

*This book is available at quantity discounts for bulk purchases.
For information, please contact info@legendarymedia.de.*

BEST PRACTICE FOR FINGERSPELLING

RIGHT HANDED PEOPLE USE RIGHT HAND

LEFT HANDED PEOPLE USE LEFT HAND

1. USE THE HAND YOU WRITE WITH
2. KEEP YOUR HAND STEADY IN ONE AREA (DO NOT BOUNCE AROUND)
3. TRY FOR A SMOOTH RHYTHM AND ACCURATE SIGNS (INSTEAD OF SPEED)
4. PAUSE BETWEEN WORDS
5. DO NOT SAY THE LETTERS WHILE FINGERSPELLING, SAY THE WORDS
6. PRACTICE, PRACTICE, PRACTICE!

① ADVERBS STARTING WITH "A"

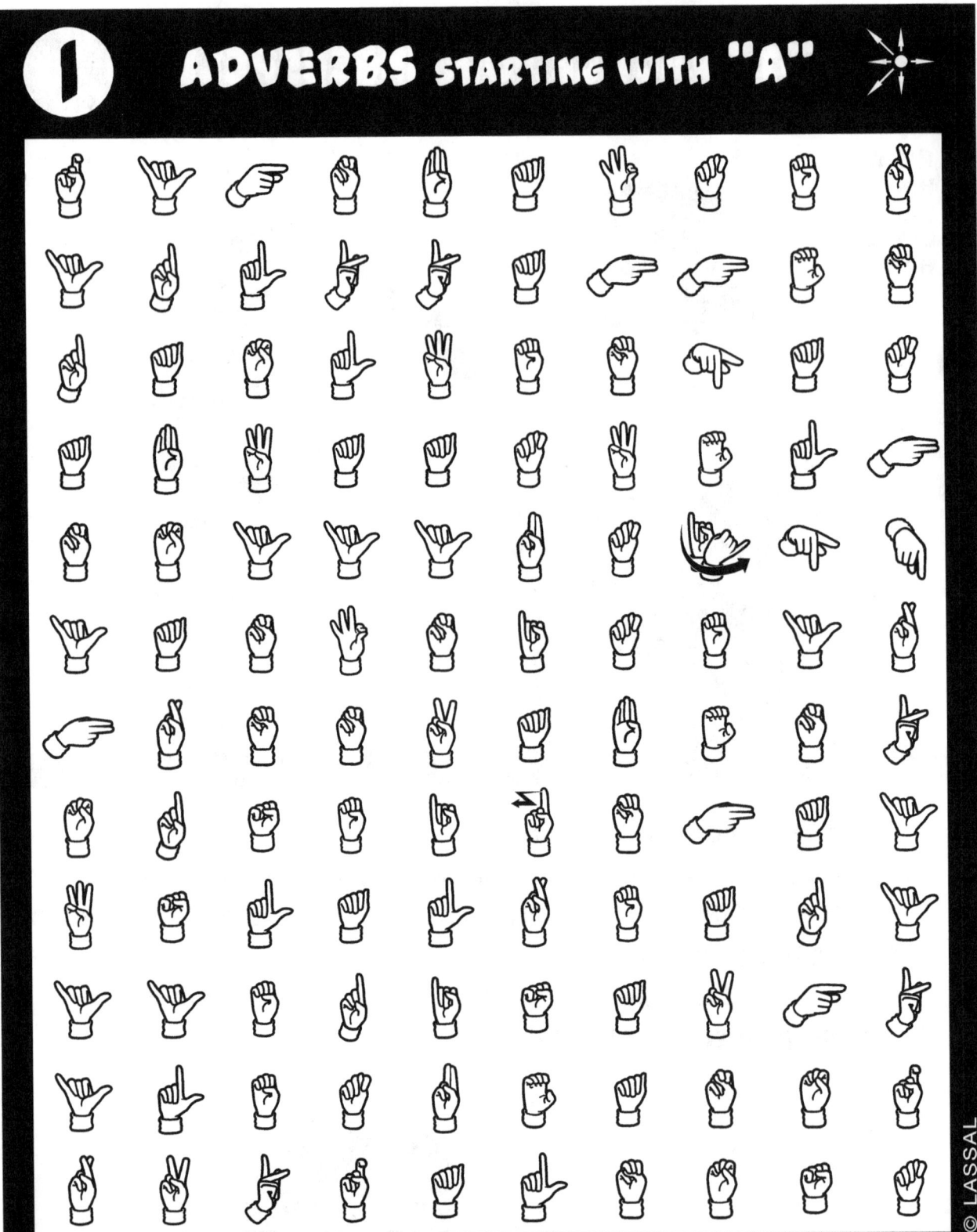

ABOARD AFTER ANYPLACE
ACTIVELY ALMOST ANYWAY
ACTUALLY ALREADY ASIDE
ACUTELY ANYHOW AWAY

2 ADVERBS starting with "B"

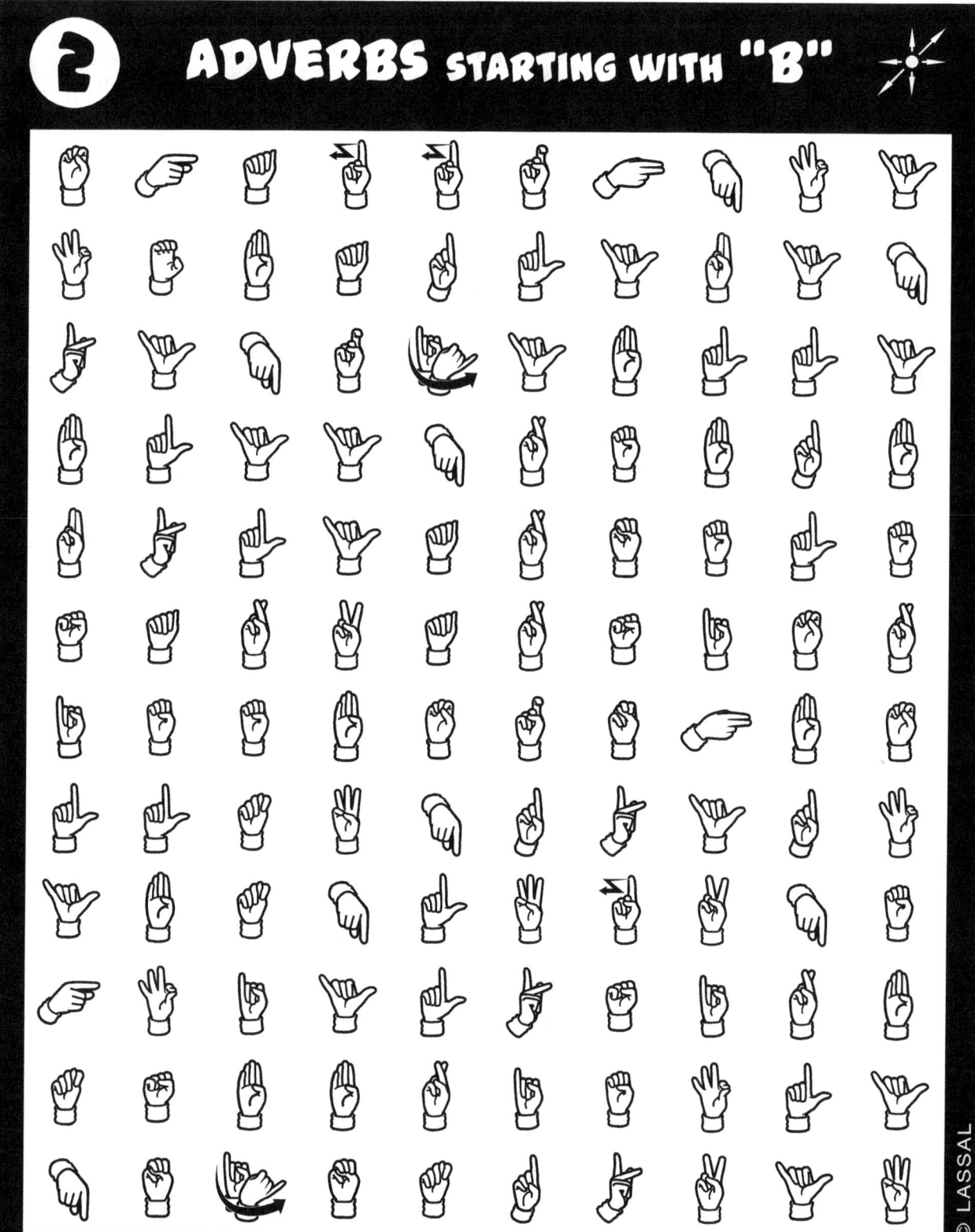

BADLY
BARELY
BEFORE
BITTERLY

BLEAKLY
BLINDLY
BOLDLY

BRAVELY
BRIEFLY
BRISKLY
BUSILY

3 ADVERBS STARTING WITH "C"

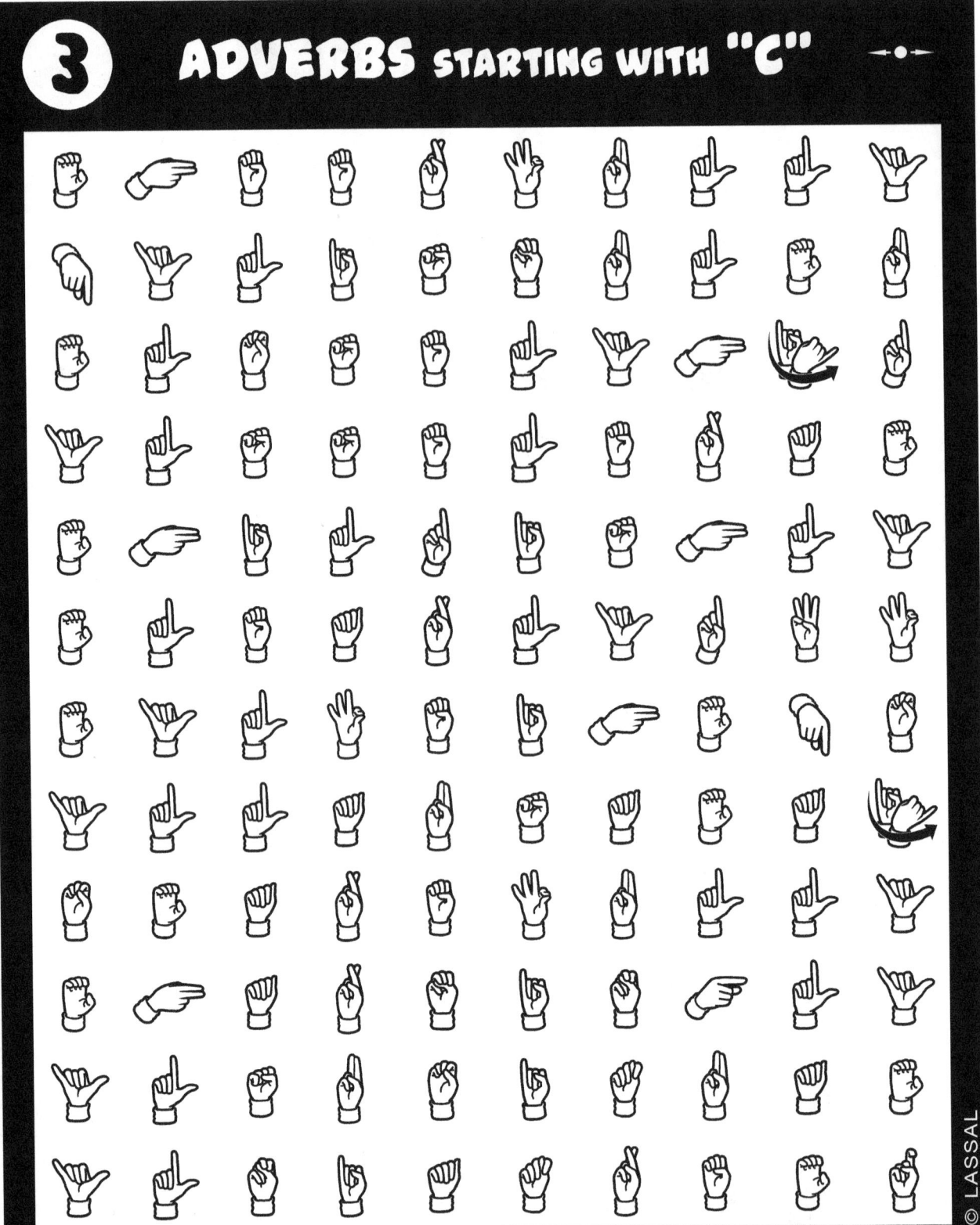

CAREFULLY	CERTAINLY	CHILDISHLY
CARELESSLY	CHARMINGLY	CLEARLY
CASUALLY	CHEERFULLY	CLOSELY
CAUTIOUSLY	CHIEFLY	CLUMSILY

4 ADVERBS STARTING WITH "D"

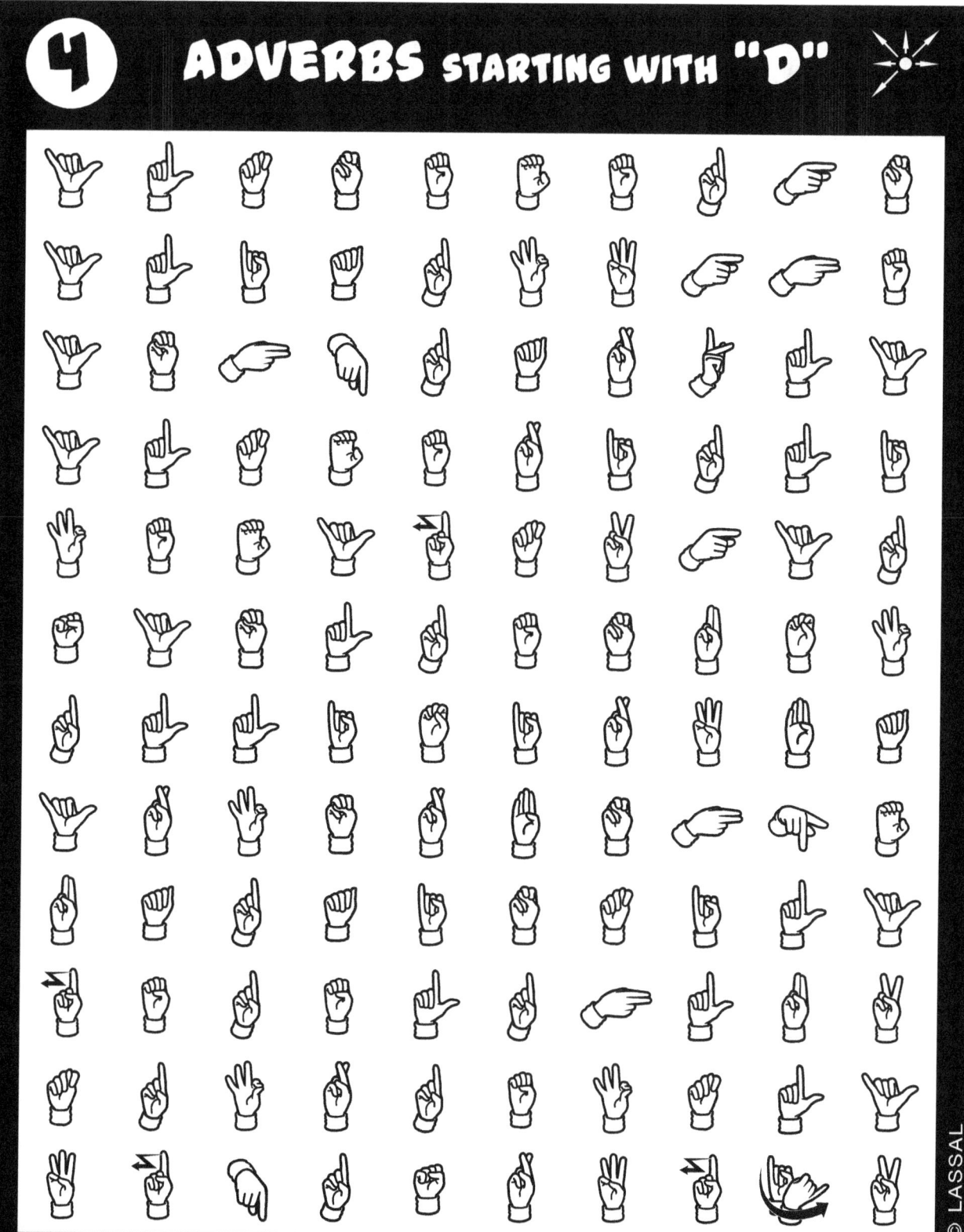

DAILY
DAINTILY
DARINGLY
DARKLY

DEARLY
DECENTLY
DEFTLY

DIMLY
DIRECTLY
DOWN
DREAMILY

5 ADVERBS STARTING WITH "E"

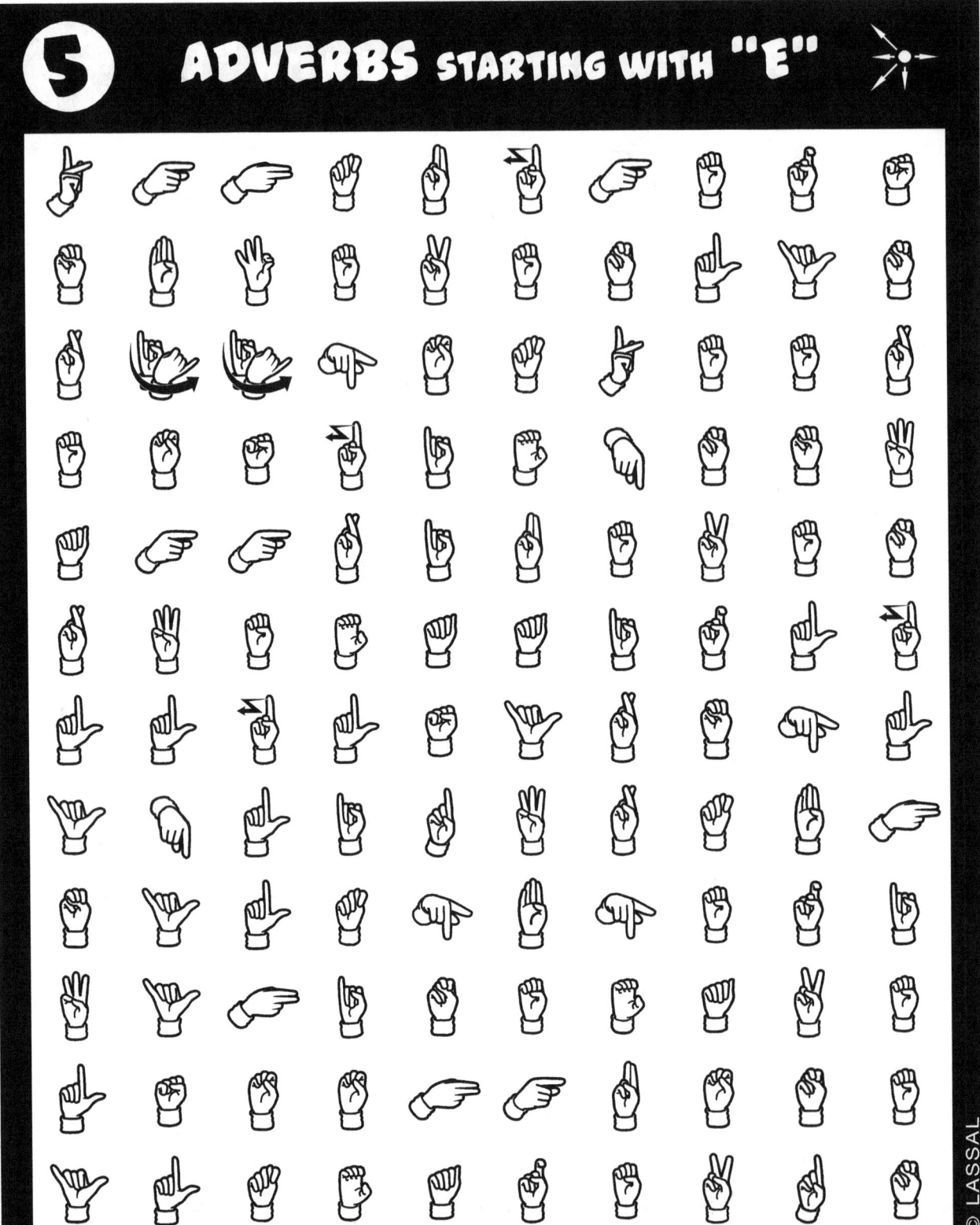

EARLY
EASILY
ENOUGH
EVERY
EVEN

EVENLY
EXACTLY
EXTRA
ENTIRELY
EQUALLY

6 ADVERBS STARTING WITH "F"

FAIRLY
FAR
FAST
FATALLY
FIERCELY

FIERY
FINALLY
FONDLY
FOREVER

FORMALLY
FORMERLY
FRANKLY
FREELY
FULLY

7 ADVERBS STARTING WITH "G"

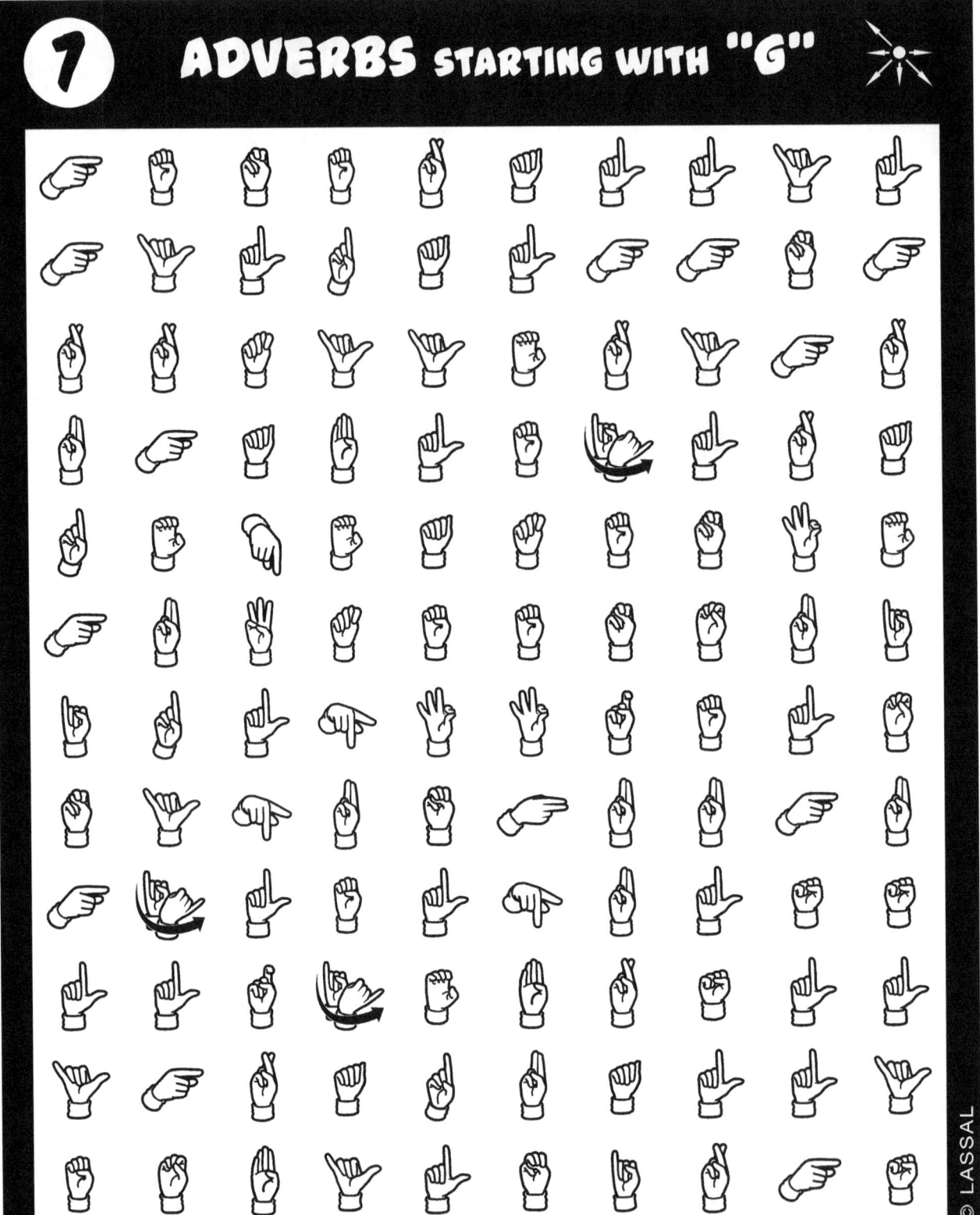

GENERALLY
GENTLY
GLADLY
GLEEFULLY
GRACEFULLY

GRACIOUSLY
GRADUALLY
GREATLY
GRIMLY
GRUDGINGLY

8 ADVERBS STARTING WITH "H"

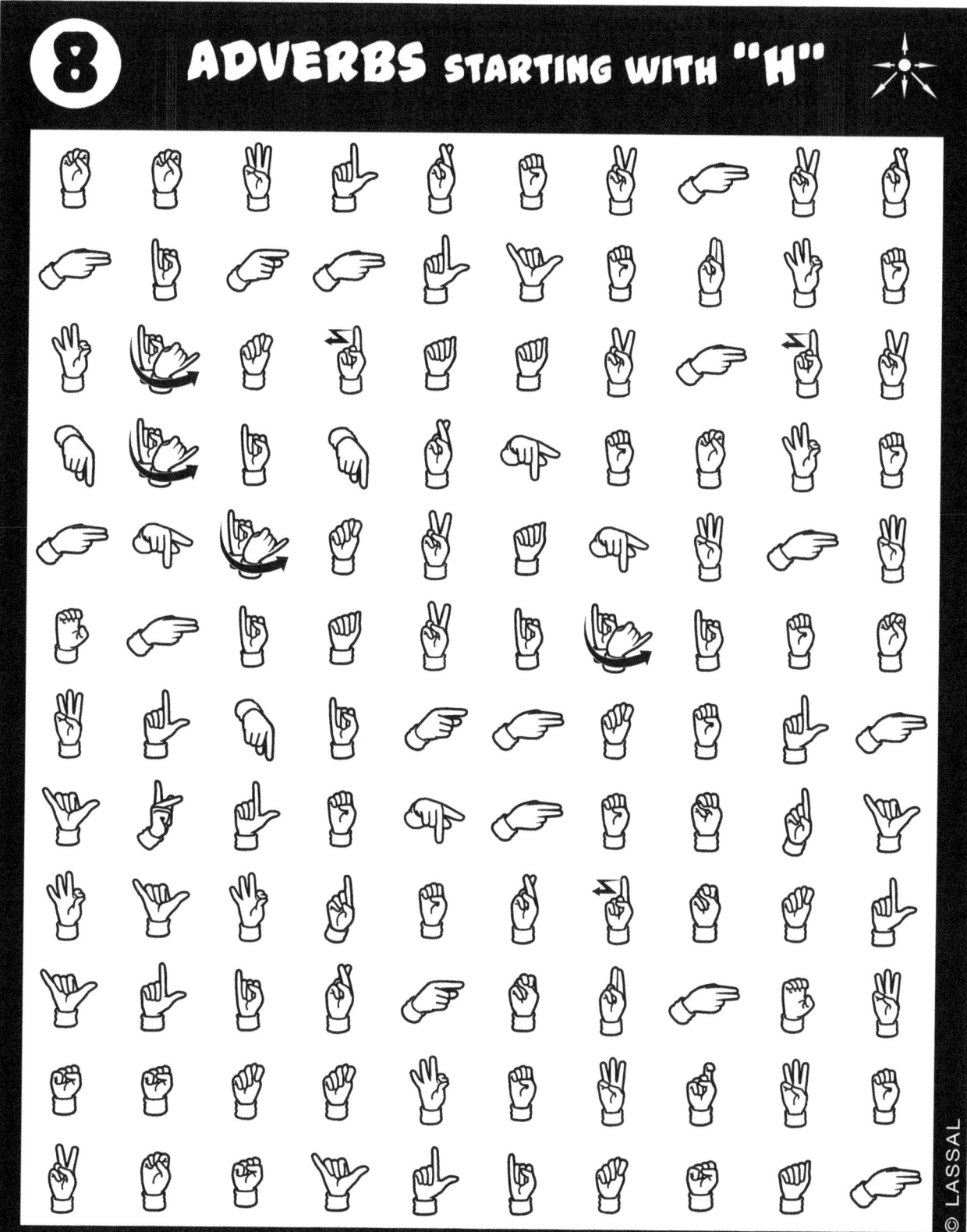

HAPPILY
HASTILY
HEARTILY
HEAVILY
HENCE

HIGHLY
HITHERTO
HOW
HOWEVER
HUNGRILY

9 ADVERBS STARTING WITH "I"

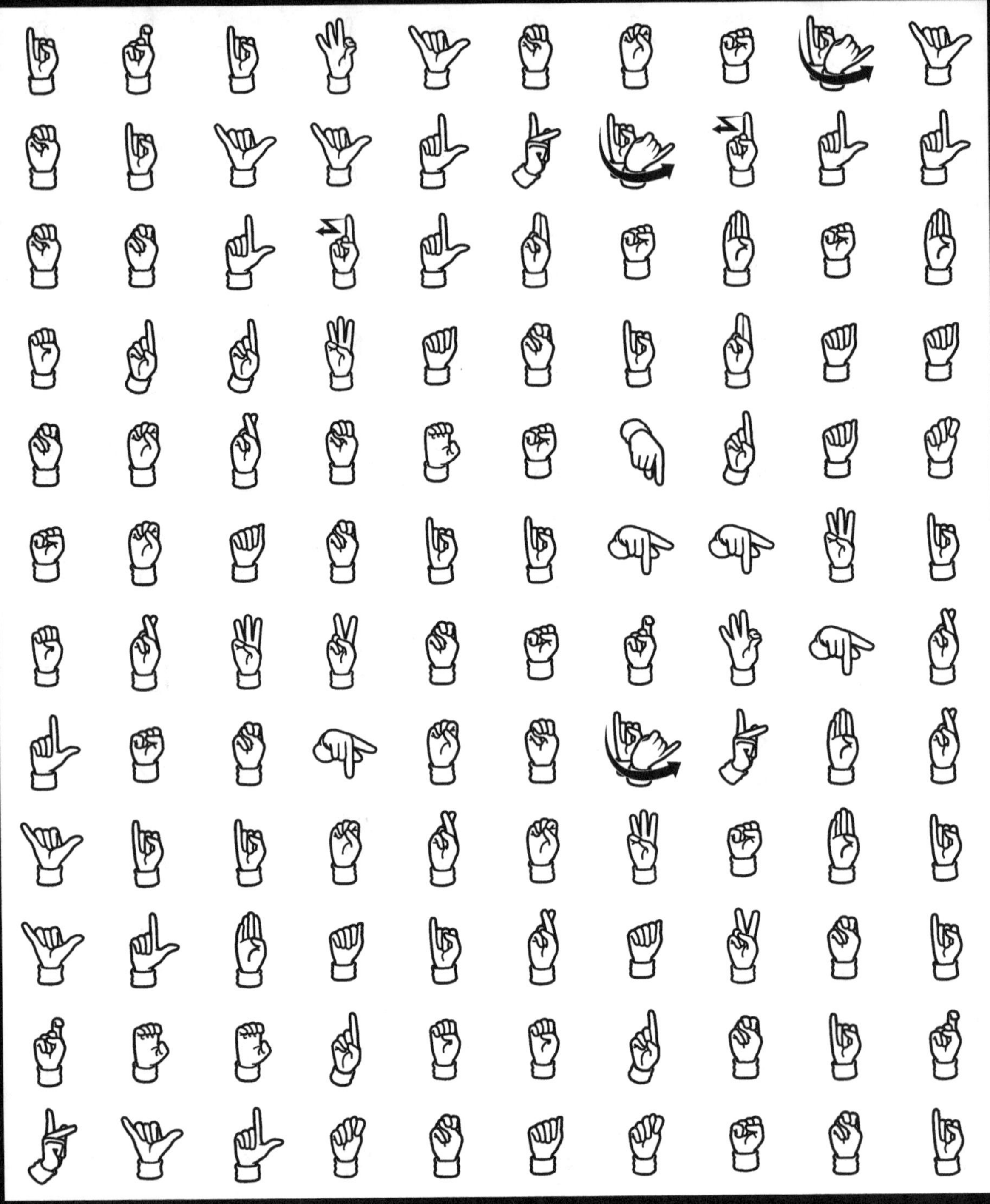

IMMENSELY
INDEED
INDOORS

INSTANTLY
INVARIABLY
INVISIBLY

INWARDLY
IRONICALLY
IRRITABLY

10 ADVERBS starting with "J"

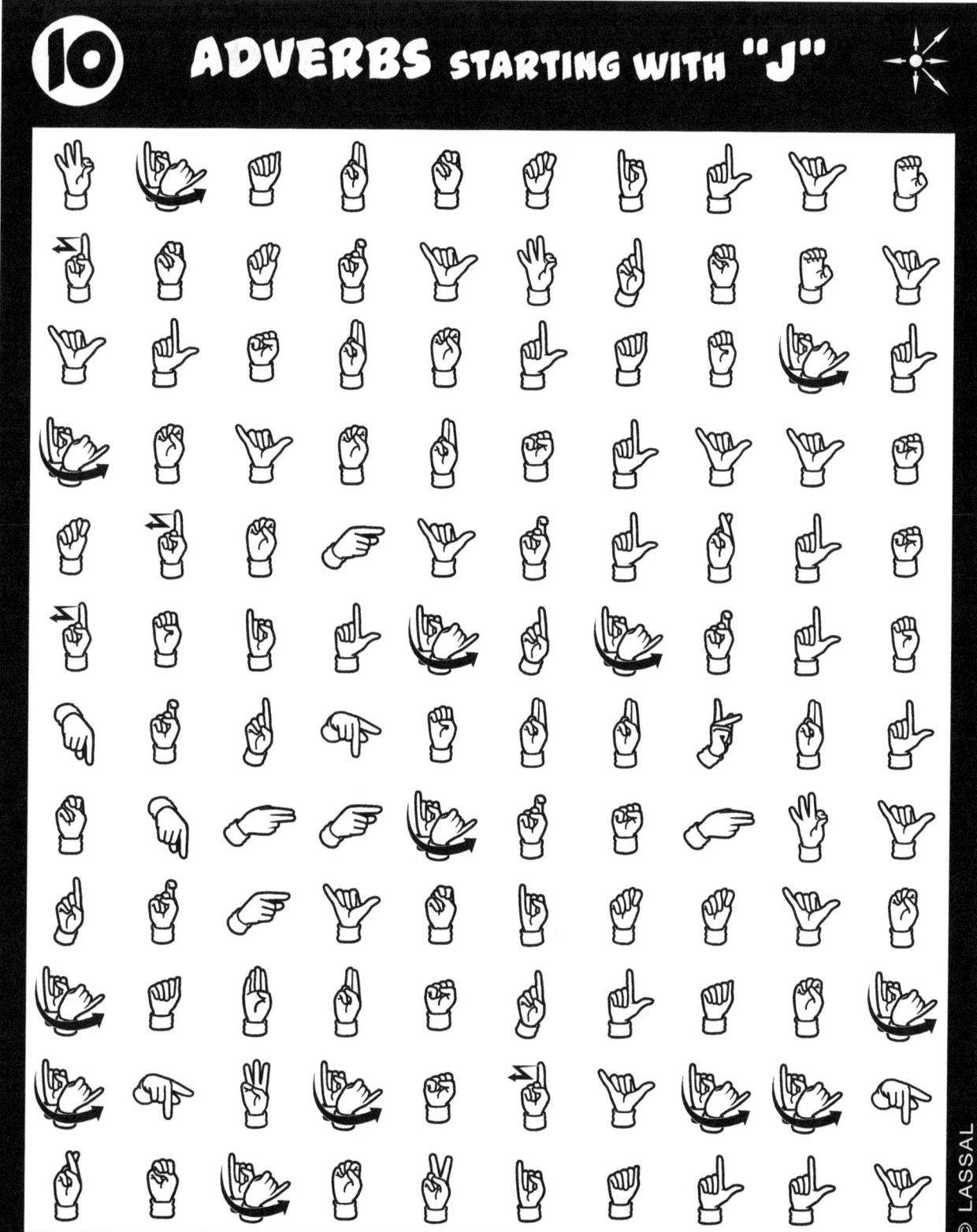

JAGGEDLY
JAUNTILY
JEALOUSLY

JOVIALLY
JOYFULLY
JOYLESSLY

JOYOUSLY
JUST
JUSTLY

11 ADVERBS STARTING WITH "K"

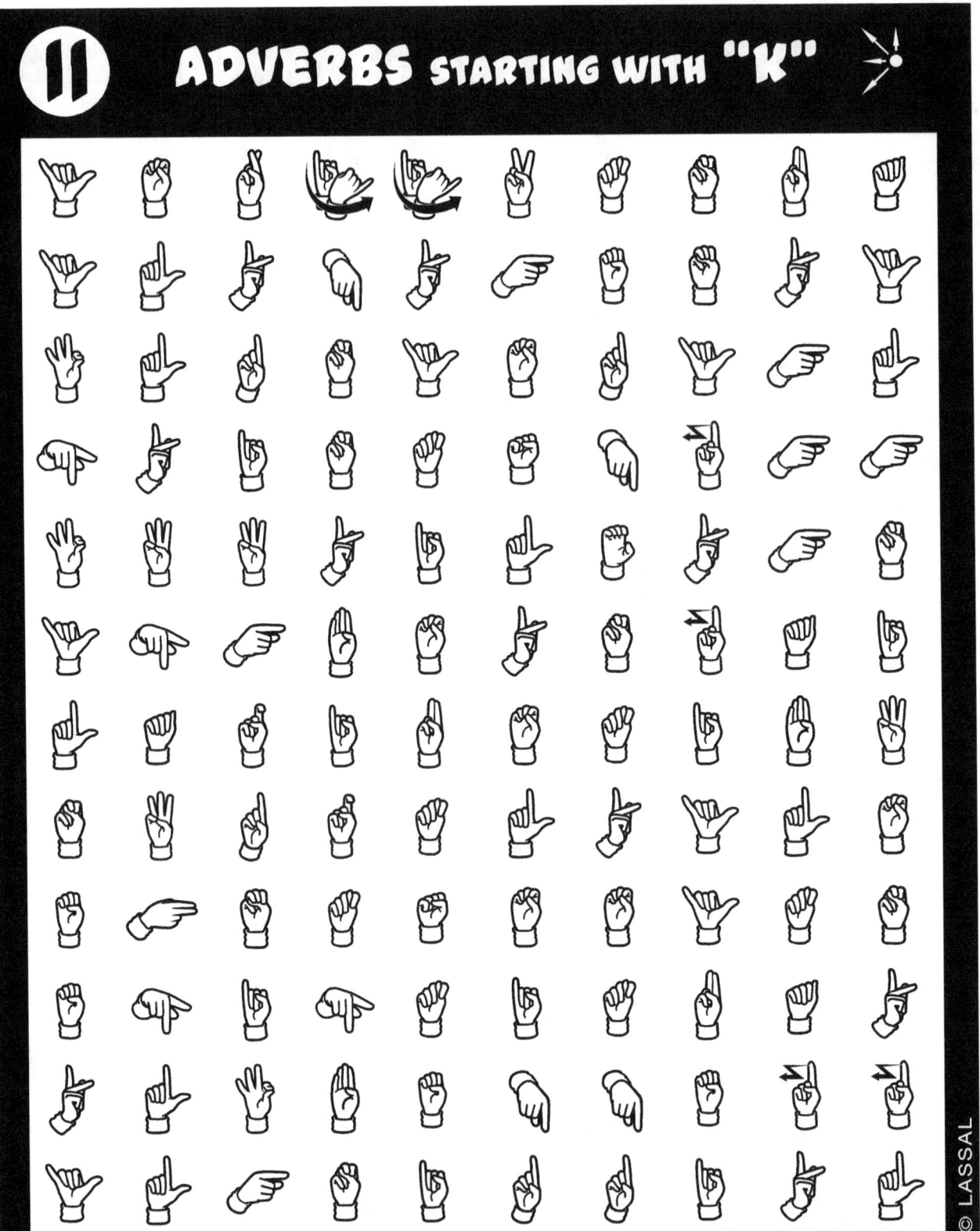

KEENLY
KIDDINGLY
KINDLY

KNOTTILY
KNOWINGLY
KOOKILY

12 ADVERBS STARTING WITH "L"

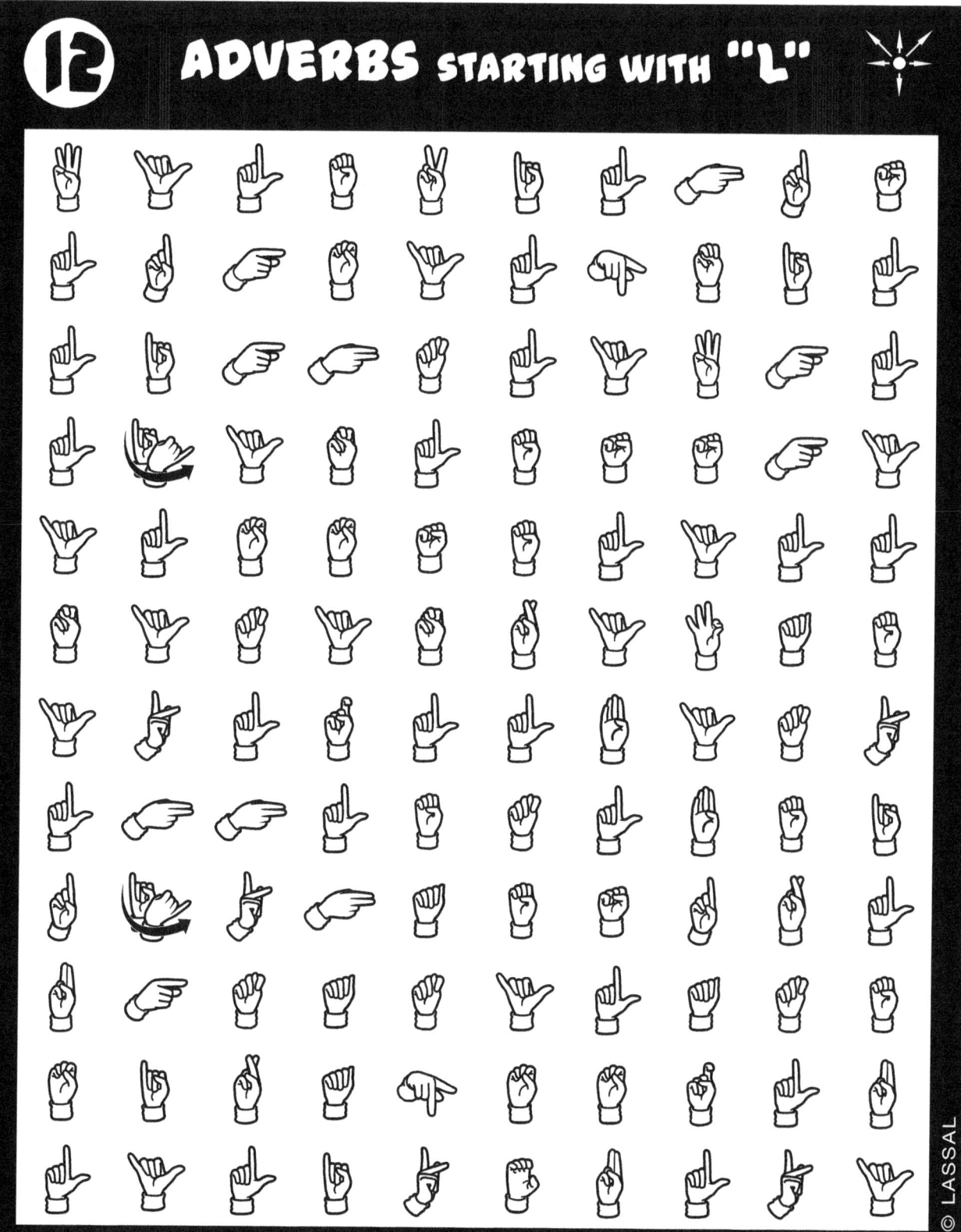

LASTLY
LATE
LATELY
LATER
LESS

LIGHTLY
LIKELY
LIMPLY
LITHELY

LIVELY
LOOSELY
LOUDLY
LOYALLY
LUCKILY

13 ADVERBS STARTING WITH "M"

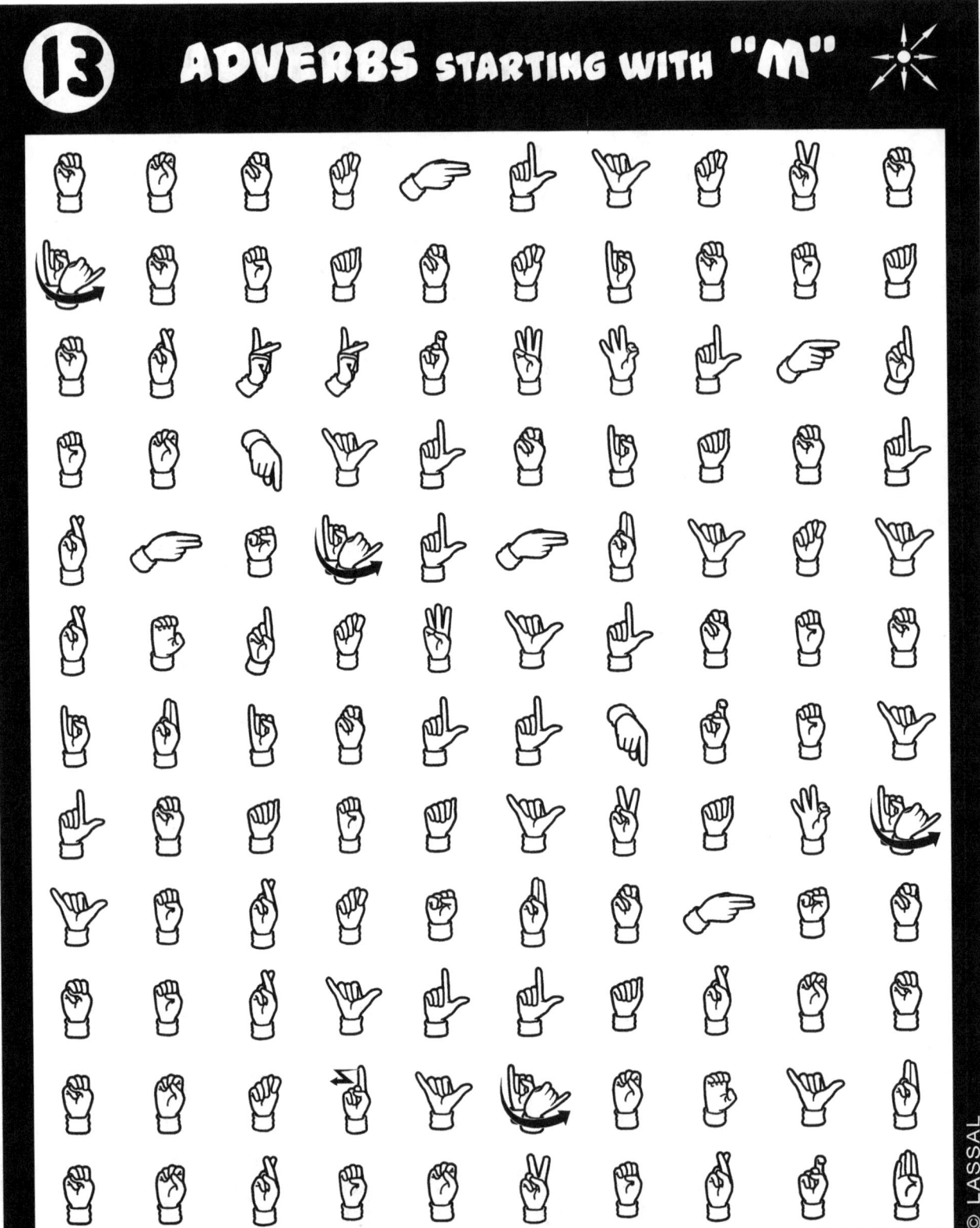

MADLY
MAINLY
MEANLY
MEANTIME

MEANWHILE
MERELY
MERRILY
MONTHLY
MORALLY

MOREOVER
MORTALLY
MOSTLY
MUCH

14 ADVERBS STARTING WITH "N"

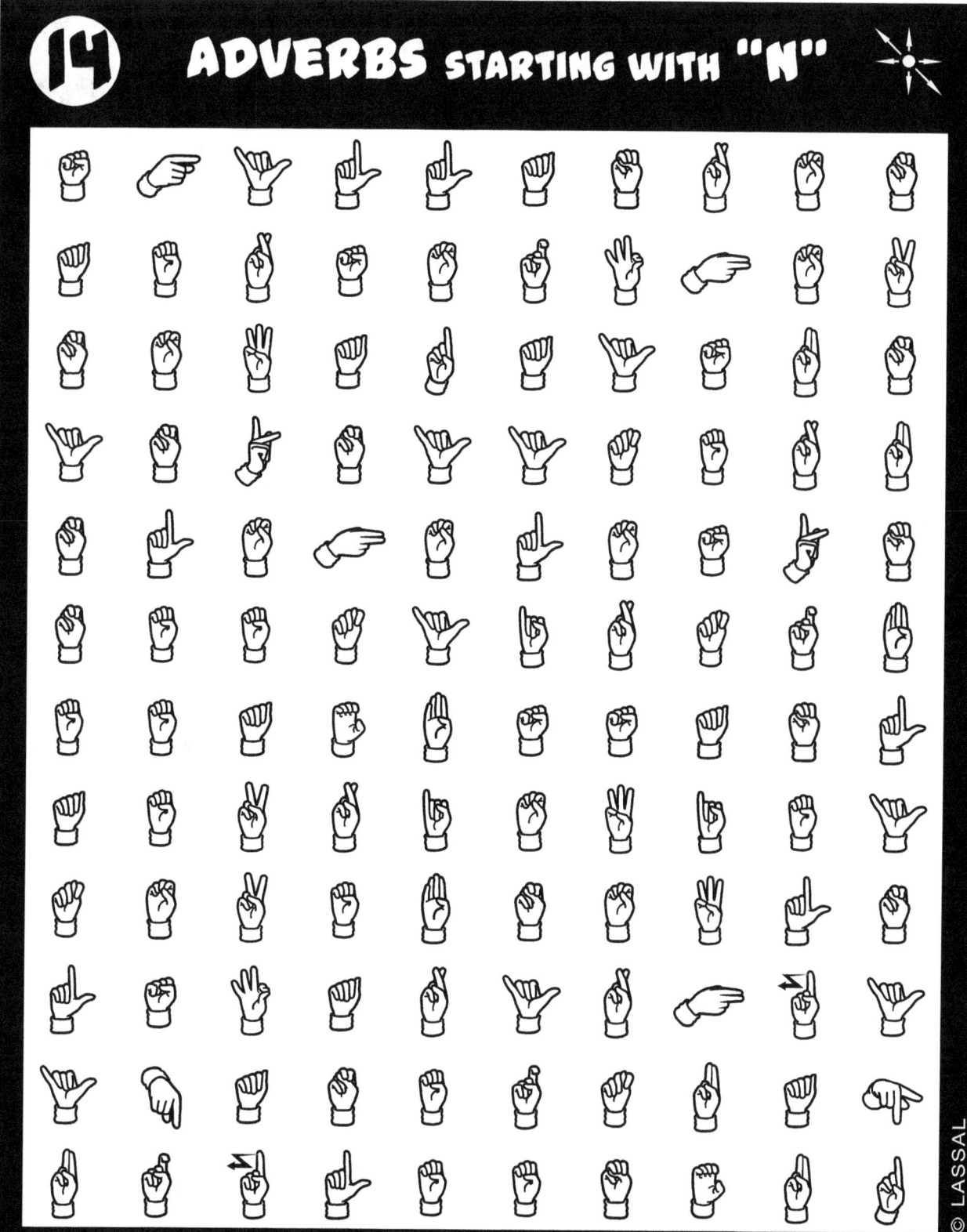

NEARBY
NEARLY
NEATLY
NEVER

NEXT
NICELY
NOISILY
NORMALLY
NOSILY

NOT
NOW
NOWADAYS
NUMBLY

15. ADVERBS STARTING WITH "O"

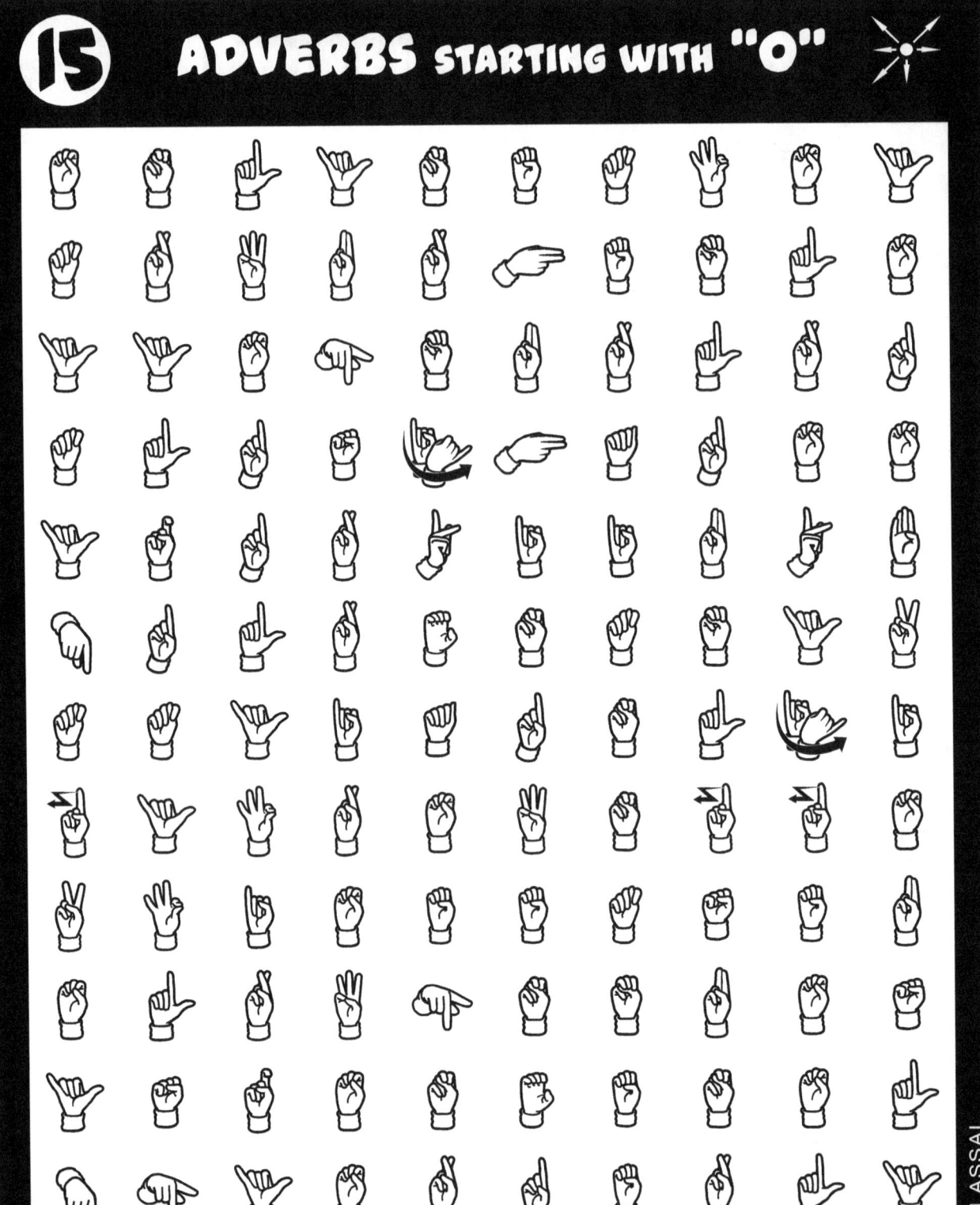

OBVIOUSLY
ODDLY
OFFICIALLY
OFTEN

ONCE
ONLY
OPENLY

ORDERLY
ORDINARILY
OUTDOORS
OUTWARDLY

16 ADVERBS STARTING WITH "P"

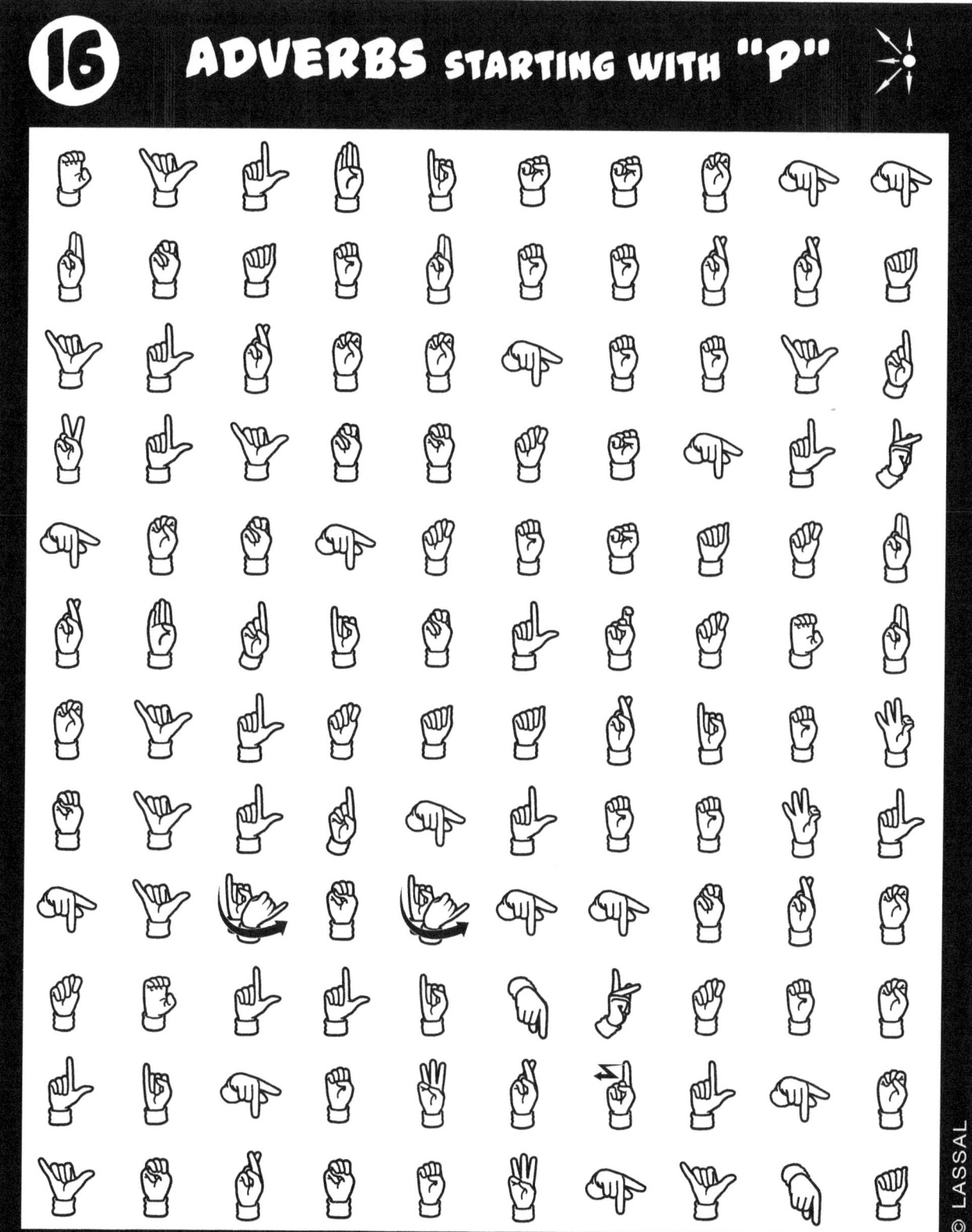

PATIENTLY
PERFECTLY
PLAINLY

POORLY
POSSIBLY
PRESENTLY

PRETTILY
PRIMLY
PROMPTLY

17 ADVERBS STARTING WITH "Q"

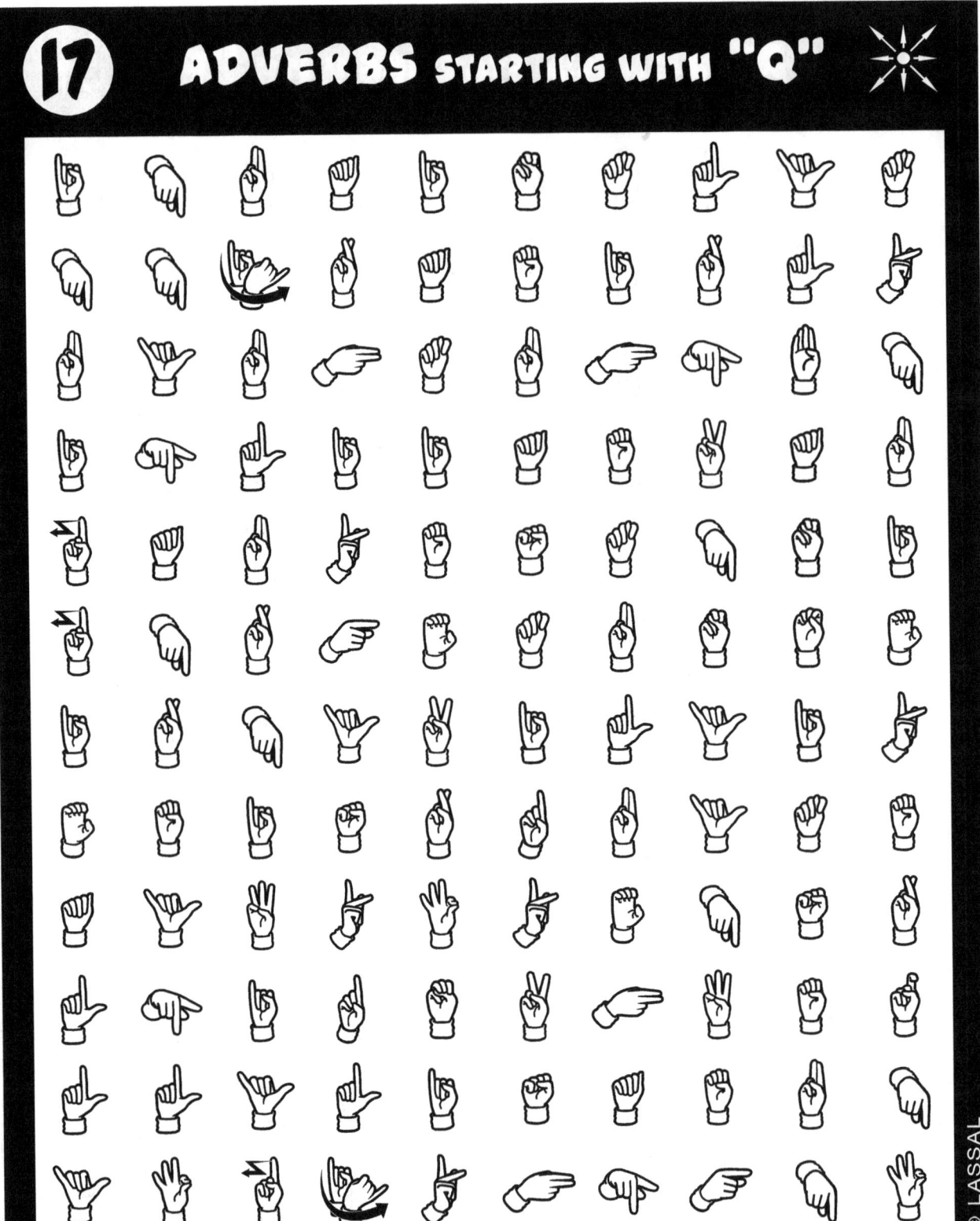

QUAINTLY
QUEASILY
QUESTIONABLY

QUICKER
QUICKLY
QUIETLY

QUIRKILY
QUITE
QUIZZICALLY

18 ADVERBS STARTING WITH "R"

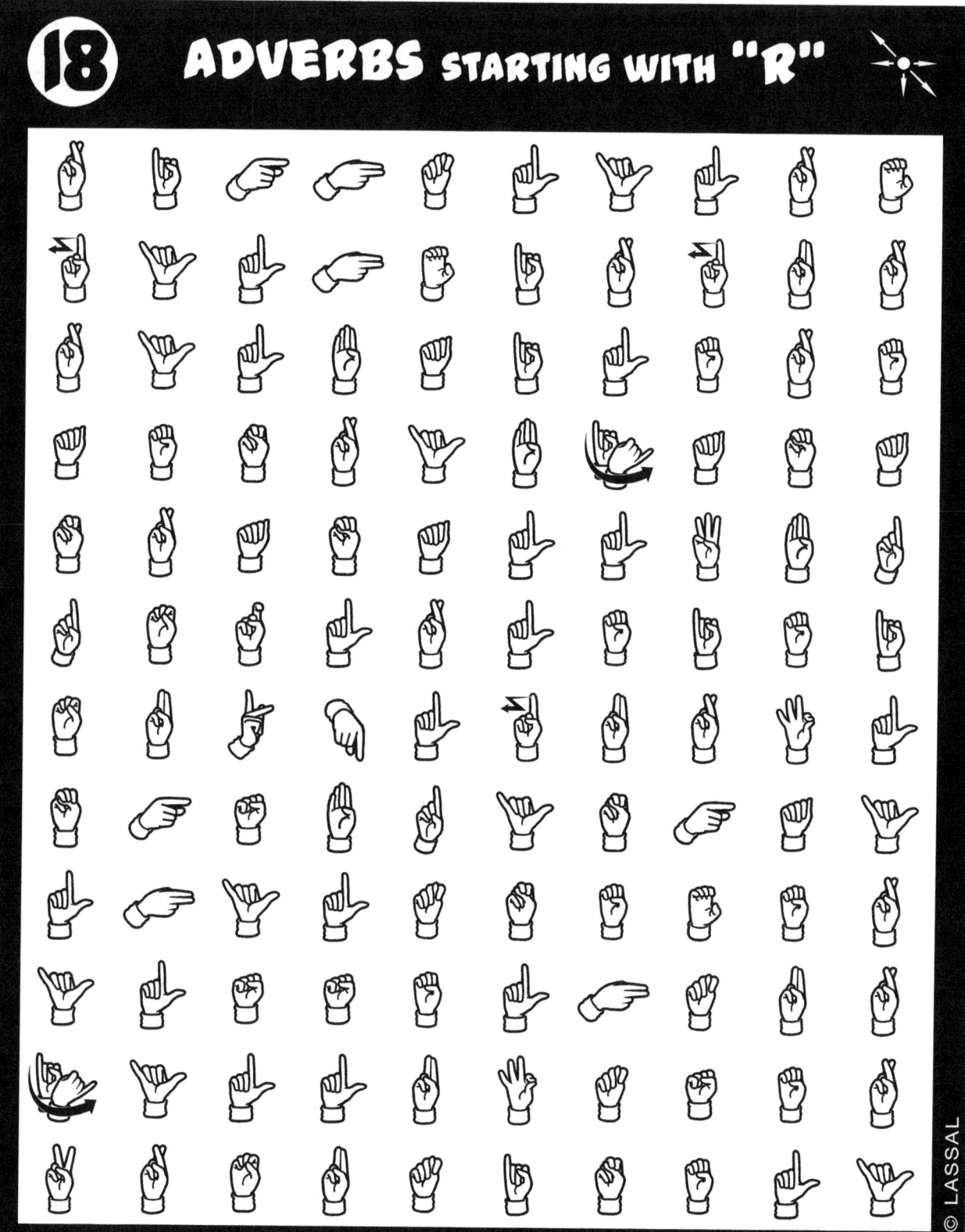

RANDOMLY
RARELY
READILY
REALLY

RECENTLY
REGULARLY
RELIABLY
RESTFULLY
RICHLY

RIGHTLY
ROUGHLY
ROUTINELY
RUTHLESSLY

19 ADVERBS STARTING WITH "S"

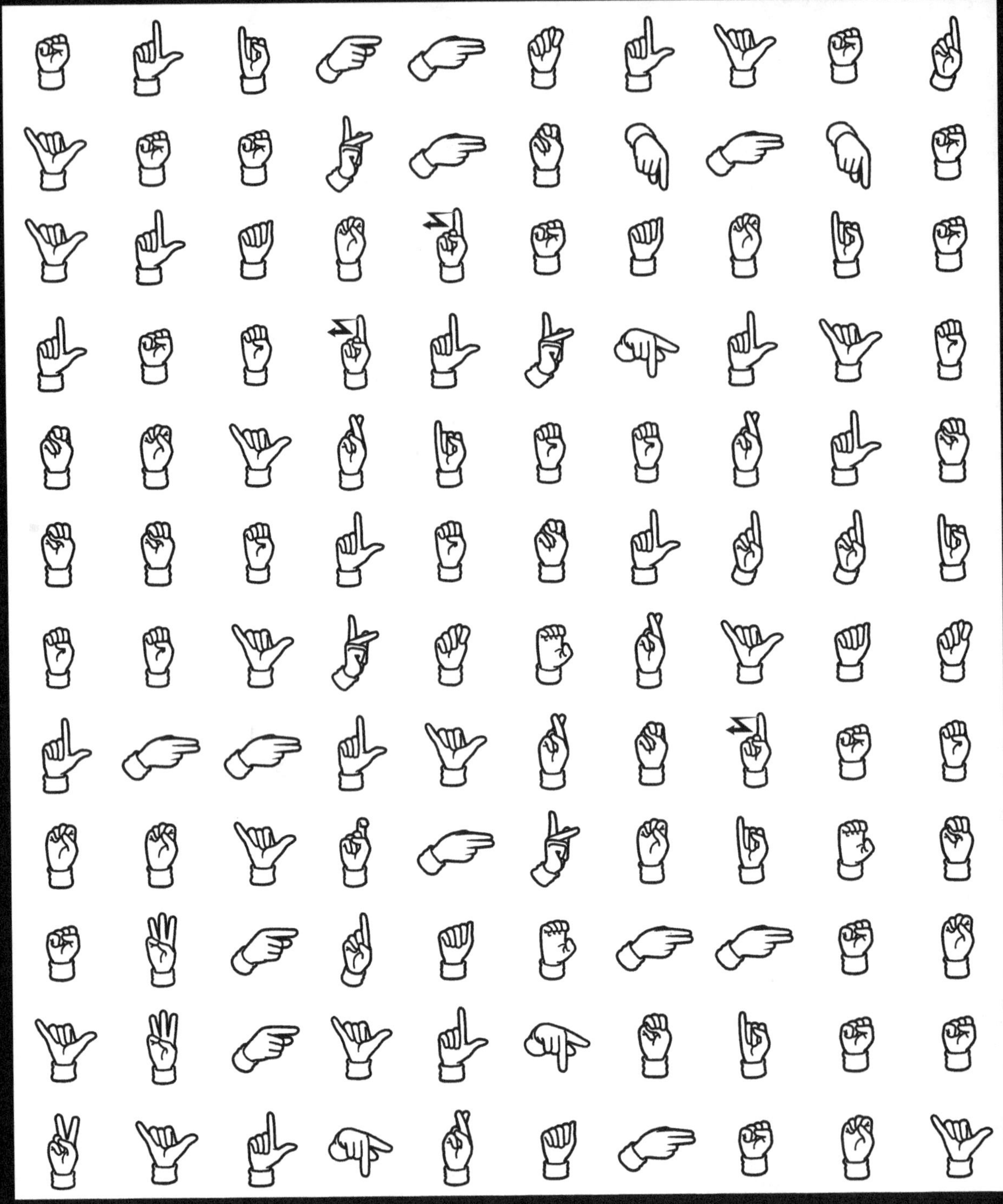

SADLY
SHAKILY
SHARPLY
SHORTLY

SILENTLY
SIMPLY
SINCERELY
SLIGHTLY

SOLELY
SOLEMNLY
SOMEHOW
SOMETIMES

20 ADVERBS STARTING WITH "S"

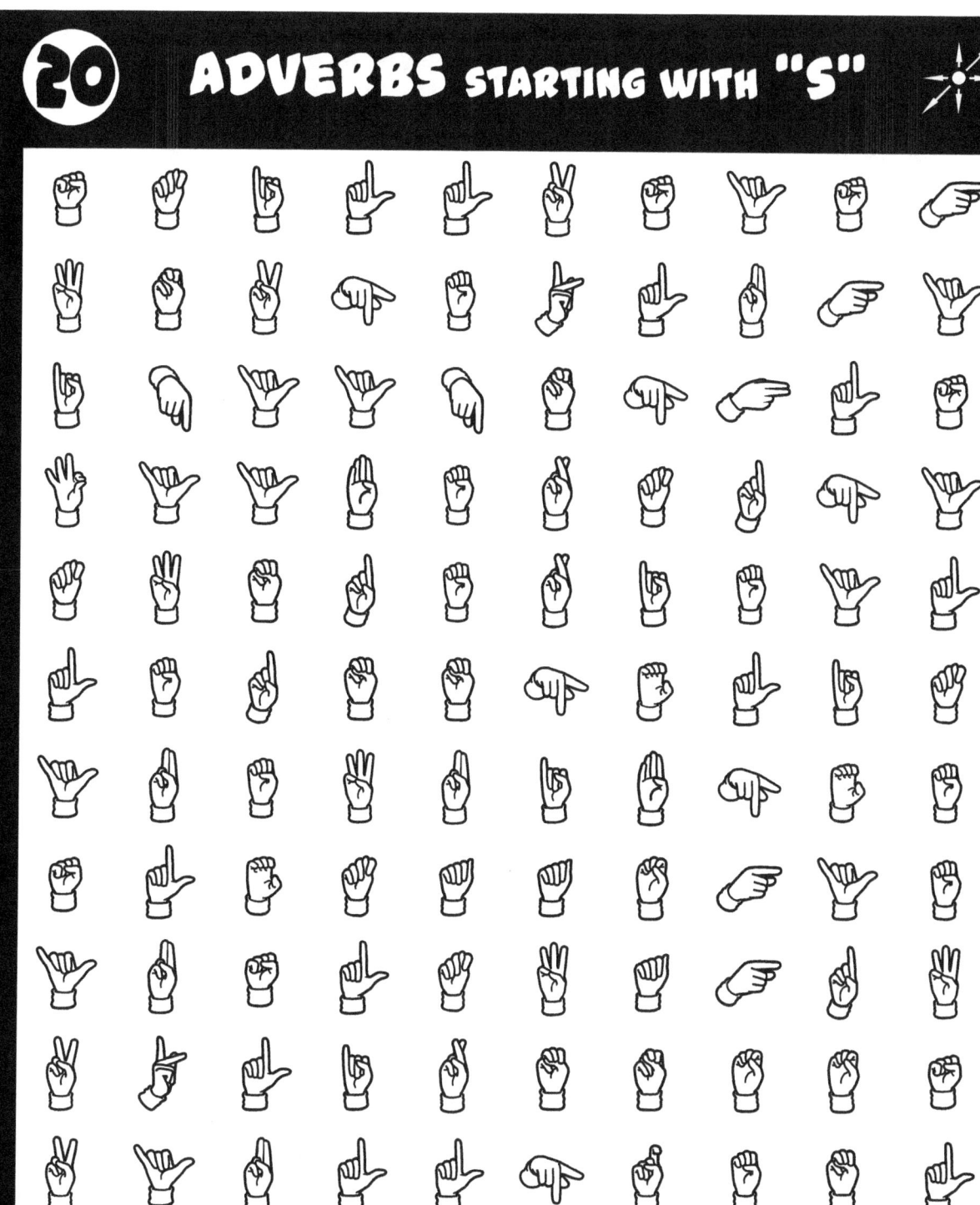

SOON
SPECIALLY
STILL

STUPIDLY
STYLISHLY
SUDDENLY
SUITABLY

SUPREMELY
SWEETLY
SWIFTLY

21 ADVERBS STARTING WITH "T"

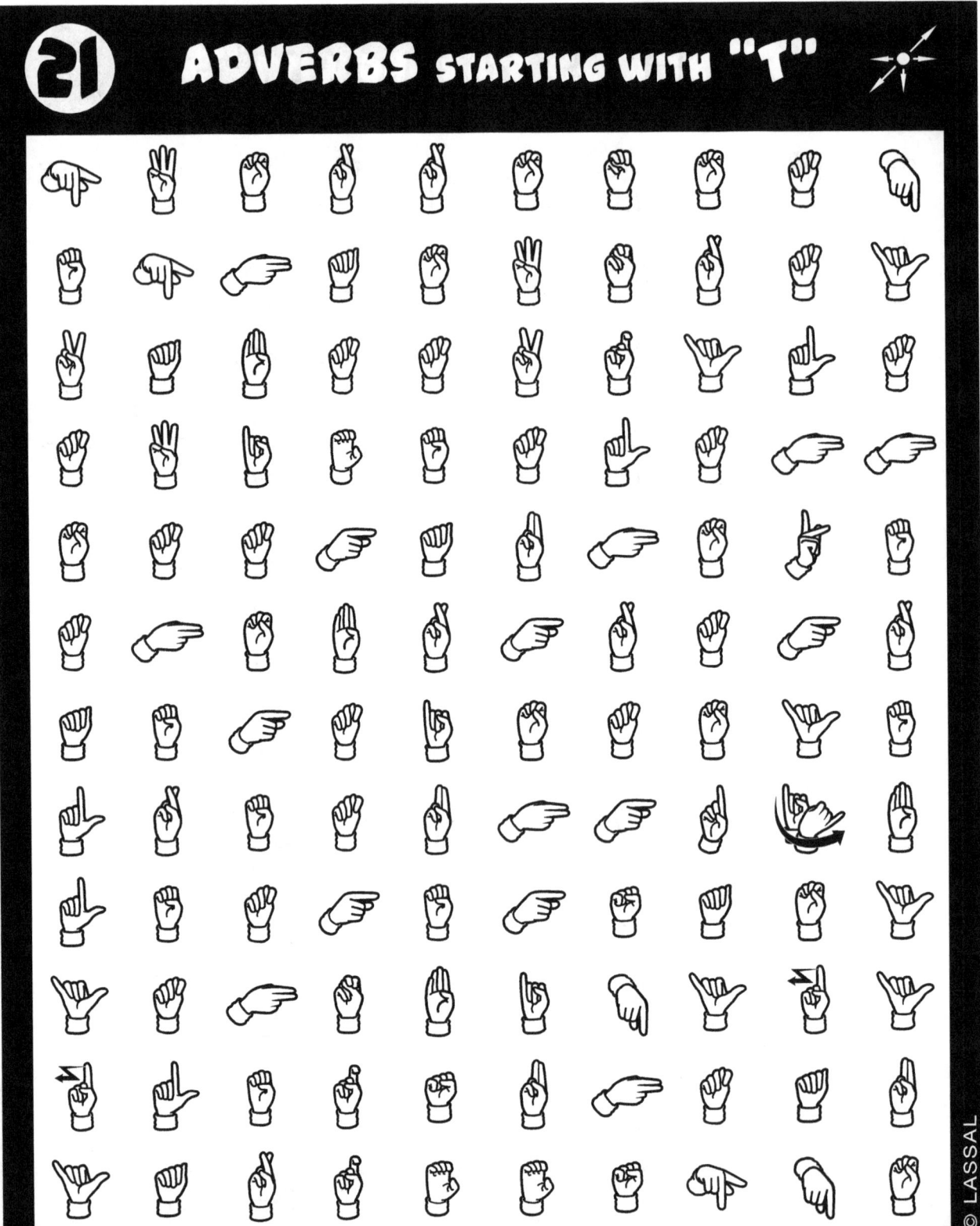

THEN
THERE
THEREBY
THOROUGHLY

THUS
TIGHTLY
TODAY
TOGETHER
TOMORROW

TOO
TOTALLY
TRULY
TWICE

22 ADVERBS STARTING WITH "U"

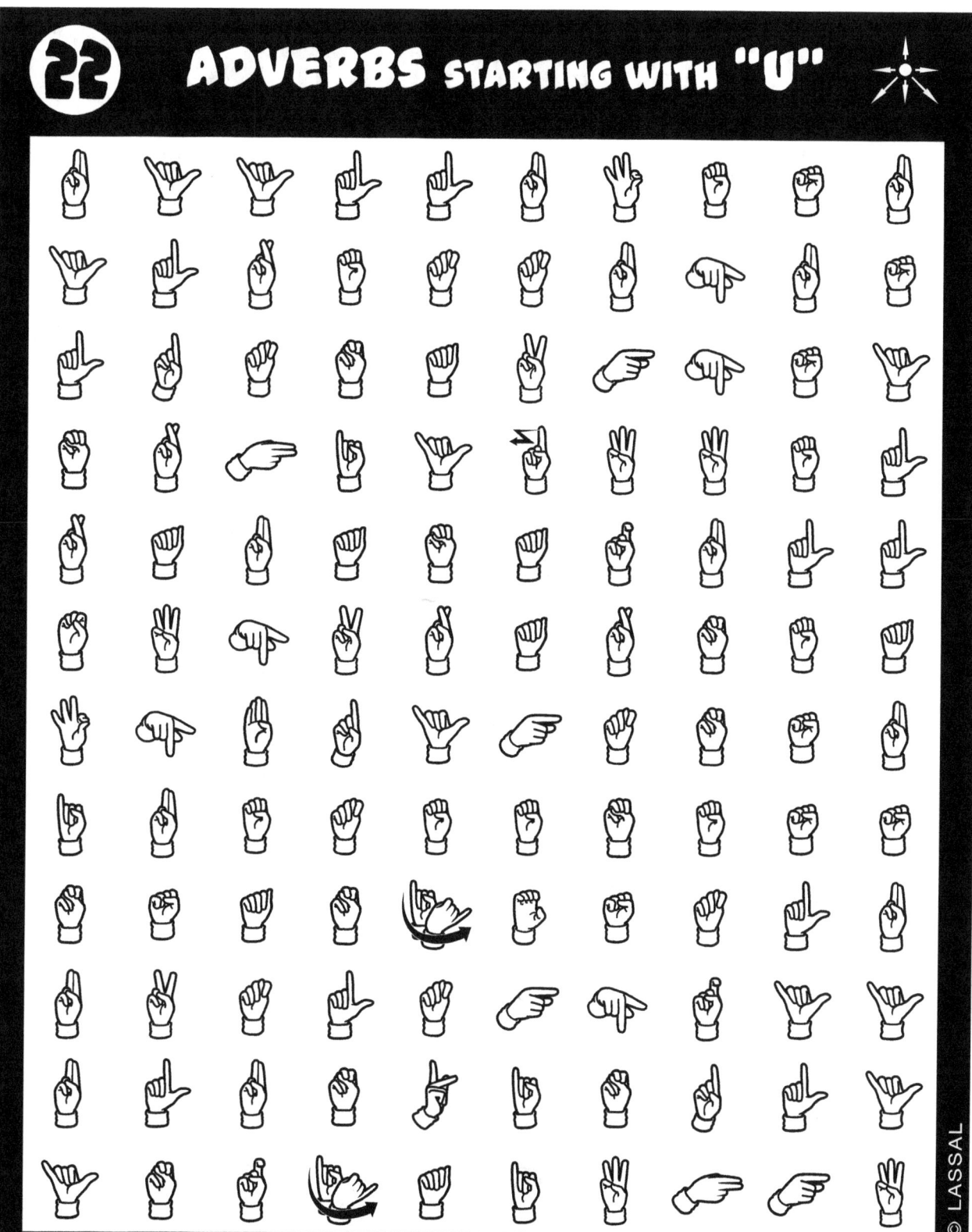

ULTIMATELY
UNIFORMLY
UNKINDLY
UPBEAT

UPWARD
UPWARDLY
URGENTLY

USEFULLY
USELESSLY
USUALLY
UTTERLY

23. ADVERBS STARTING WITH "V"

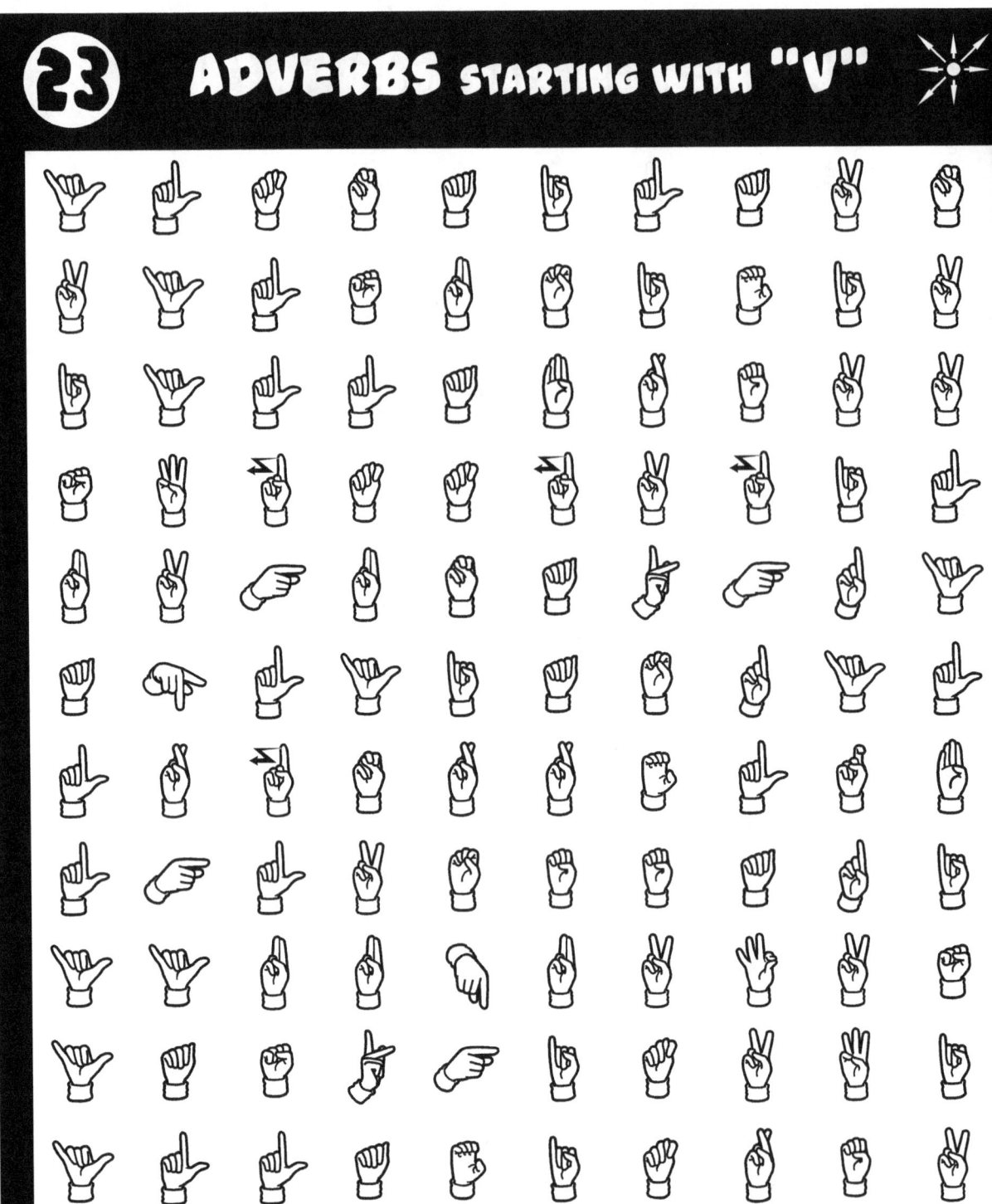

VACANTLY
VAGUELY
VAINLY
VALIANTLY

VASTLY
VERBALLY
VERTICALLY
VERY

VICIOUSLY
VIGOROUSLY
VISIBLY
VISUALLY

24 ADVERBS STARTING WITH "W"

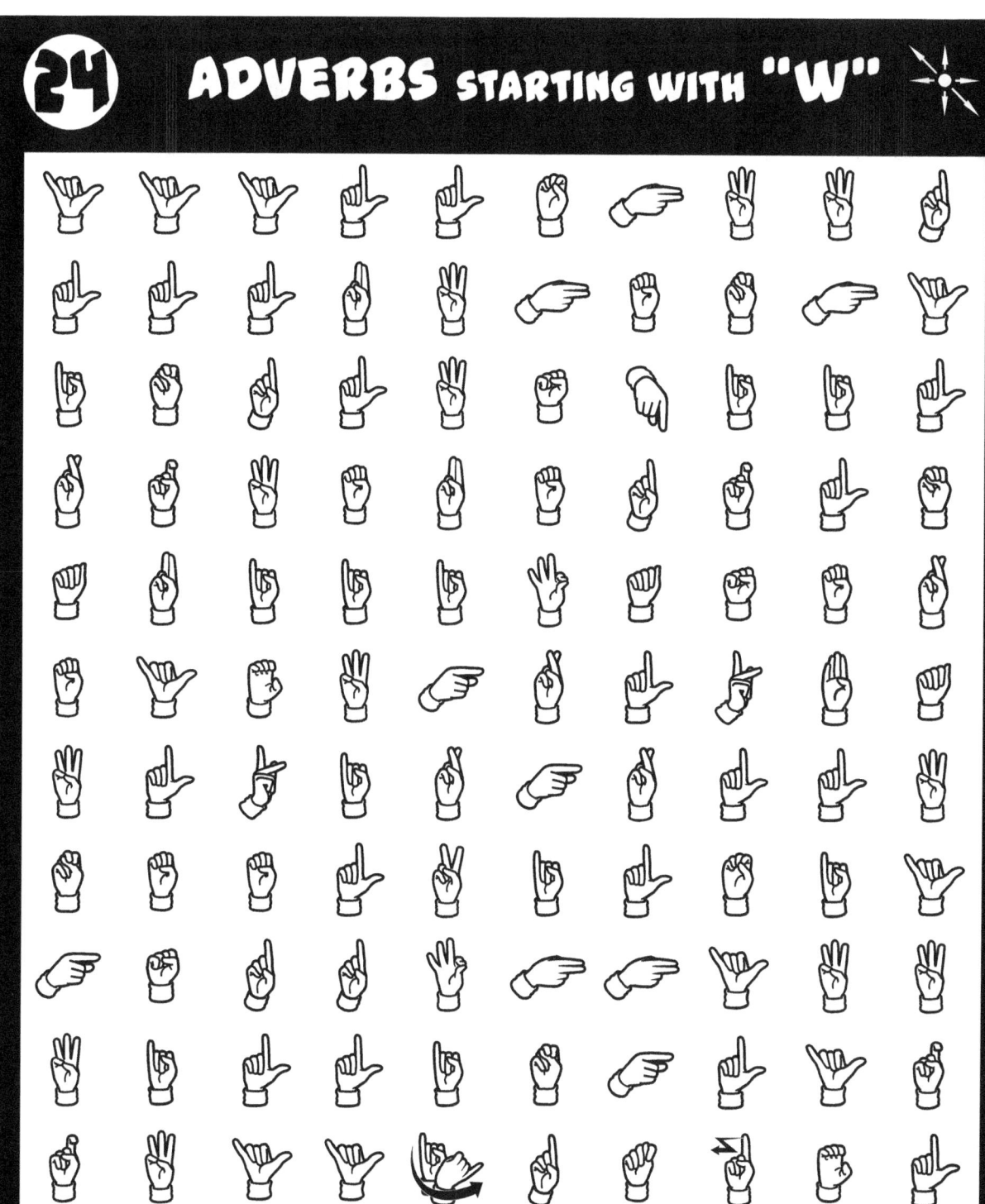

WARMLY
WEAKLY
WEARILY
WHEN
WHILE

WHOLLY
WICKEDLY
WIDELY
WIGGLY

WILDLY
WILLFULLY
WILLINGLY
WISELY
WORRIEDLY

25 ADVERBS STARTING WITH "Y", "Z"

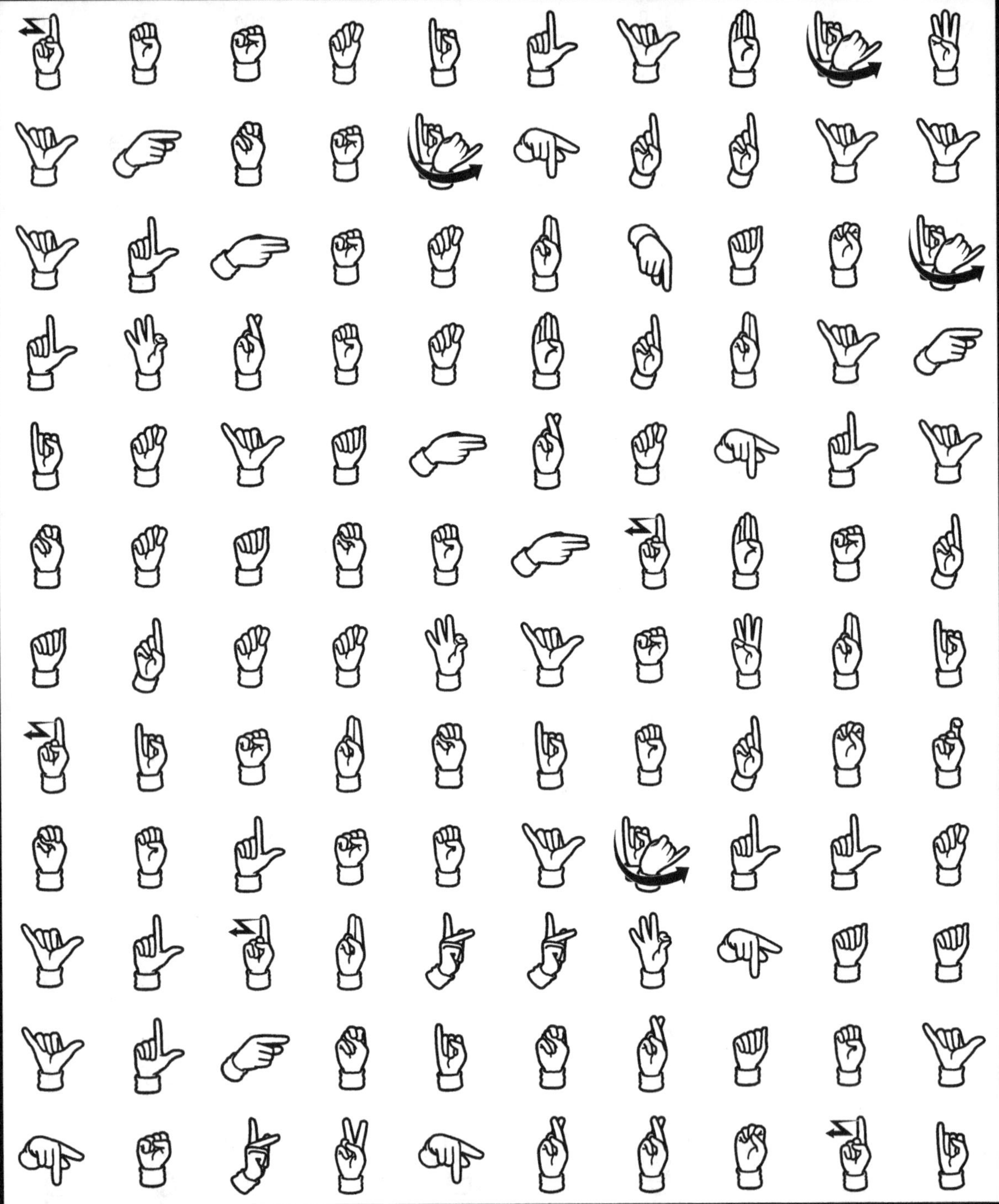

YEARLY
YEARNINGLY
YESTERDAY
YET

YOUTHFULLY
ZANILY
ZEALOUSLY
ZESTILY

26 ADVERBS of CERTAINTY

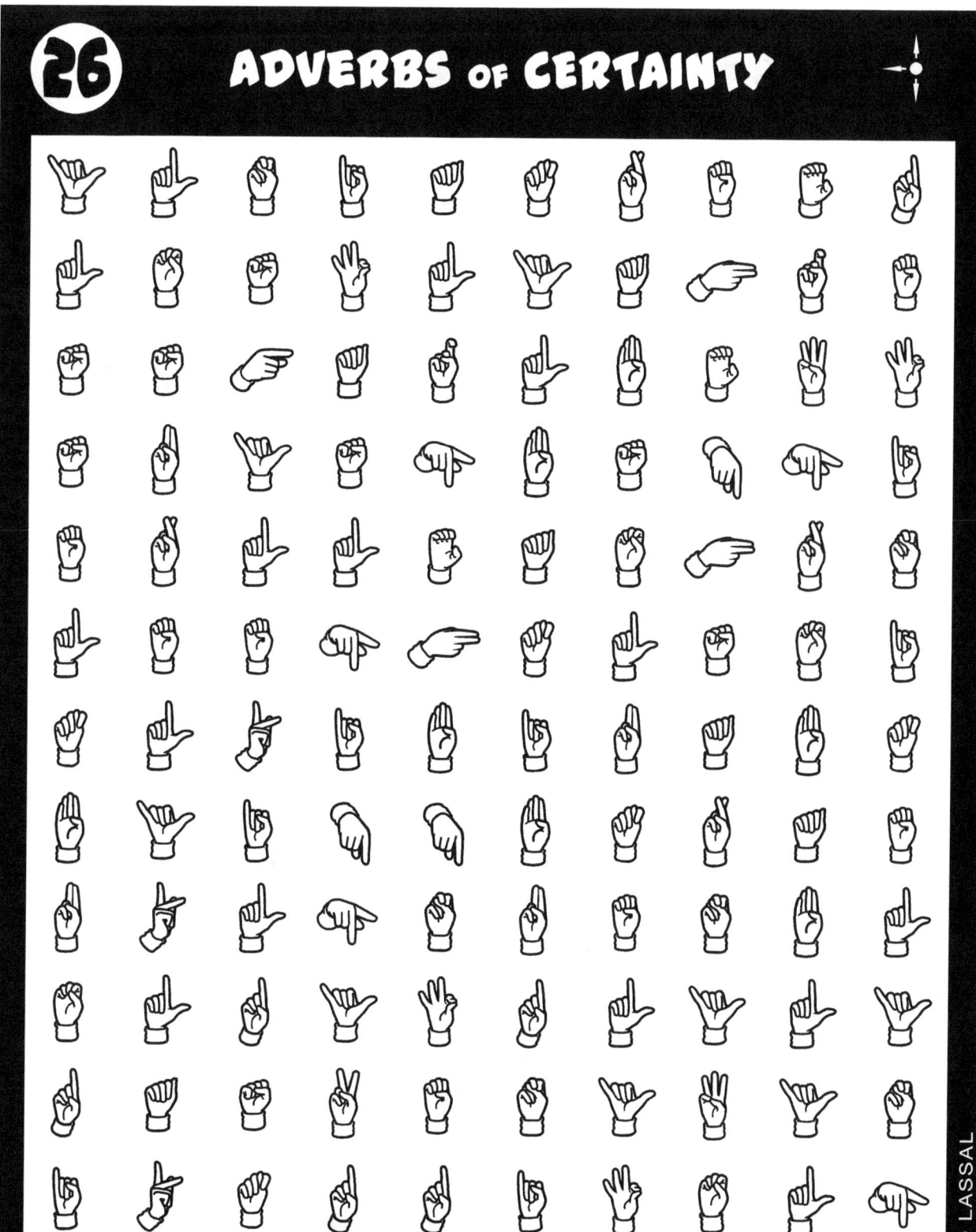

ABSOLUTELY
CERTAINLY
DEFINITELY
DOUBTLESSLY

INDUBITABLY
LIKELY
PROBABLY
SURELY

ADVERBS of DEGREE

ALMOST	JUST	THOROUGHLY
BARELY	LESS	TOO
COMPLETELY	NEARLY	TOTALLY
EXTREMELY	QUITE	VERY
HARDLY	SCARCELY	WEAKLY

28 ADVERBS of TIME

AFTER	PUNCTUALLY	TODAY
BEFORE	RECENTLY	TOMORROW
LATER	STILL	YESTERDAY
OFTEN	SUDDENLY	YET

29 ADVERBS of FREQUENCY

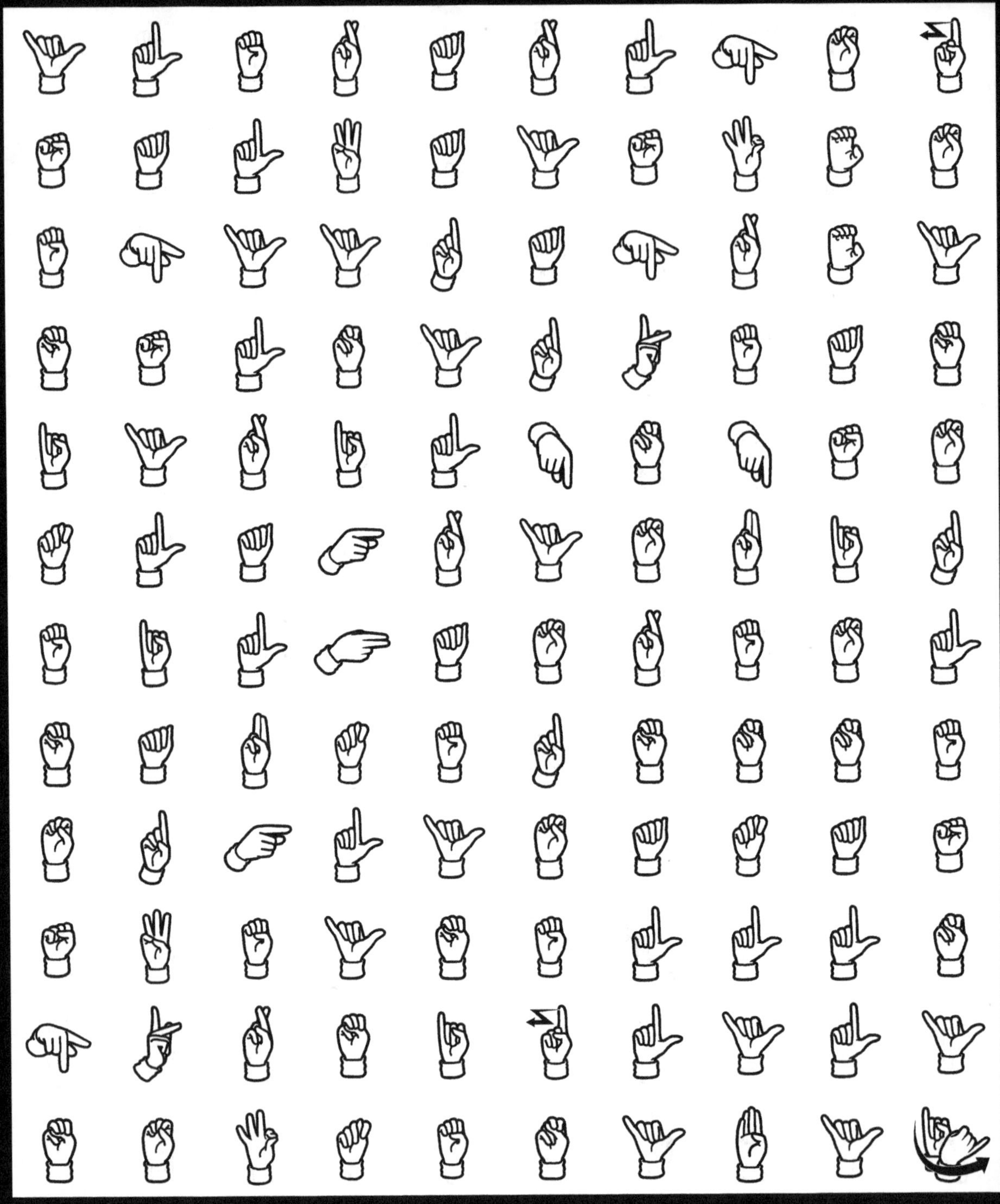

ALWAYS
DAILY
FREQUENTLY
NIGHTLY

NORMALLY
OCCASIONALLY
OFTEN
RARELY

REGULARLY
SELDOM
SOMETIMES
YEARLY

30 ADVERBS of MANNER

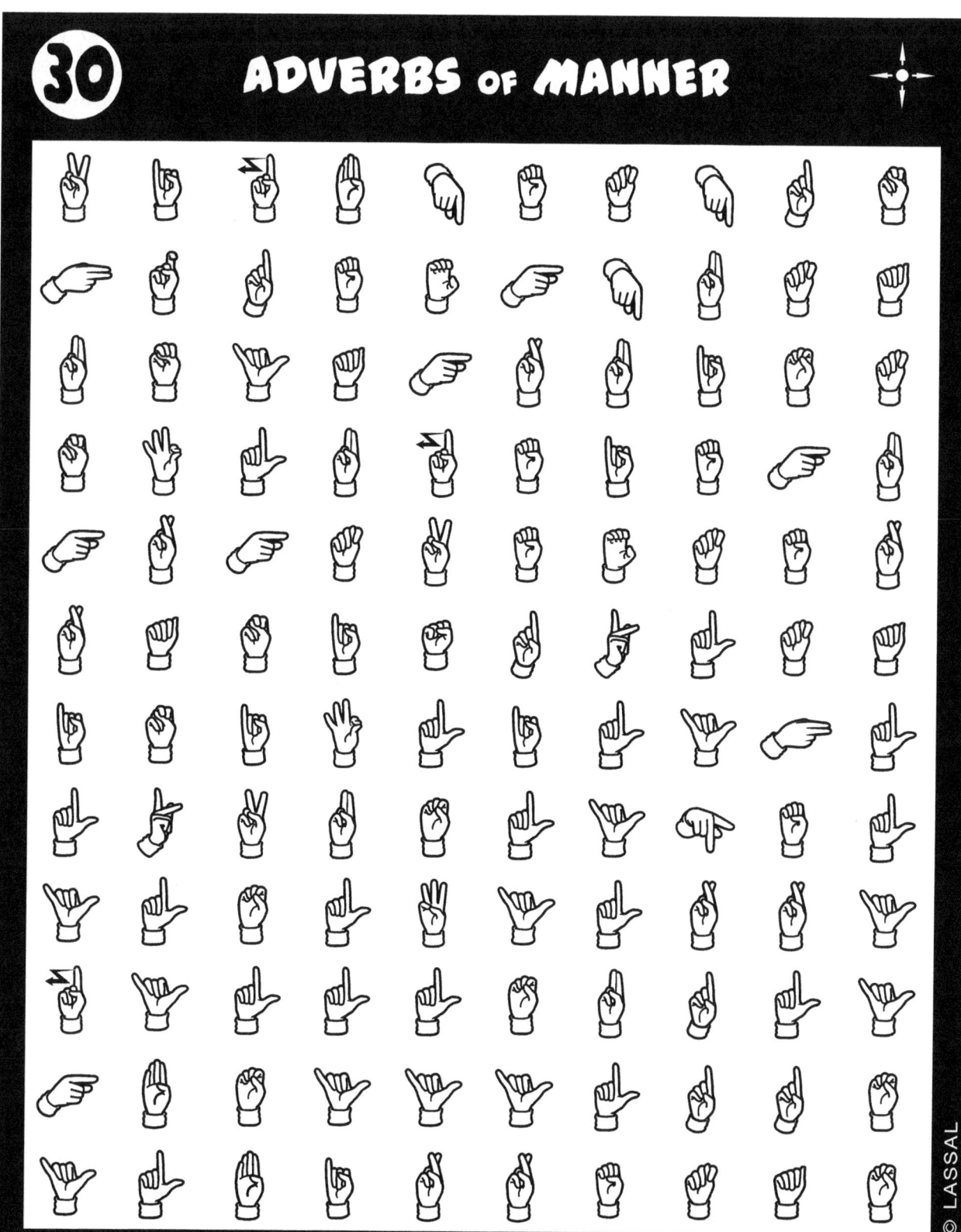

BEAUTIFULLY
FRANKLY
GREEDILY
HUNGRILY

LOUDLY
LOVINGLY
NATURALLY
ODDLY
QUICKLY

QUIETLY
SLOWLY
TERRIBLY
TOGETHER

31 ADVERBS of PLACE

ABROAD
BACKWARD
DOWNWARD
EVERYWHERE
FAR

FORWARDS
HERE
HOME
HOMEWARD
NEARBY
OUTSIDE

OUTWARDLY
SOUTHWARD
THERE
UP
UPWARD

32 ADVERBS MIX 1

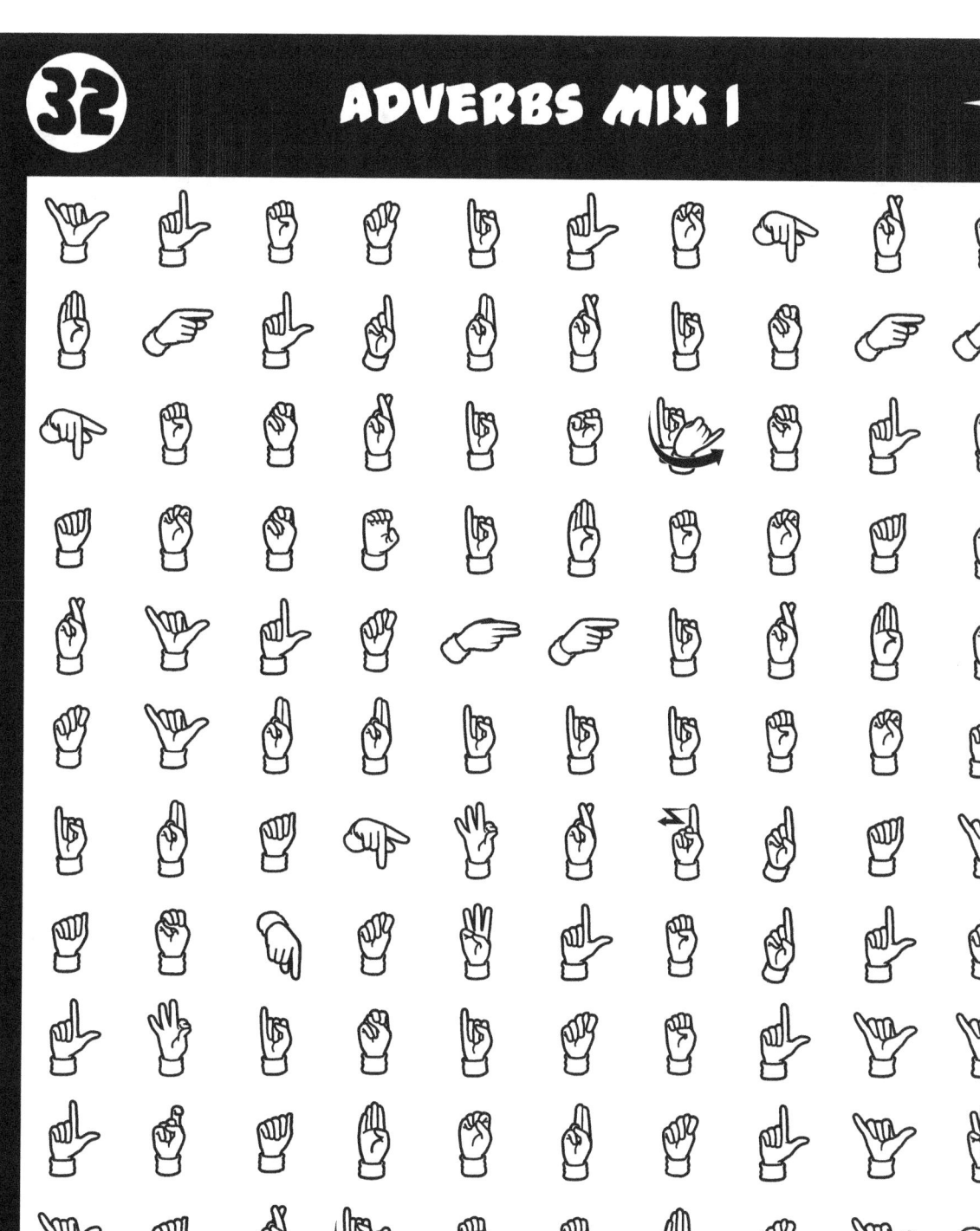

ABOUT	HOURLY
BRIGHTLY	MORE
DURING	PARTIALLY
ENTIRELY	POLITELY
FINITELY	RIGIDLY

33 ADVERBS MIX 2

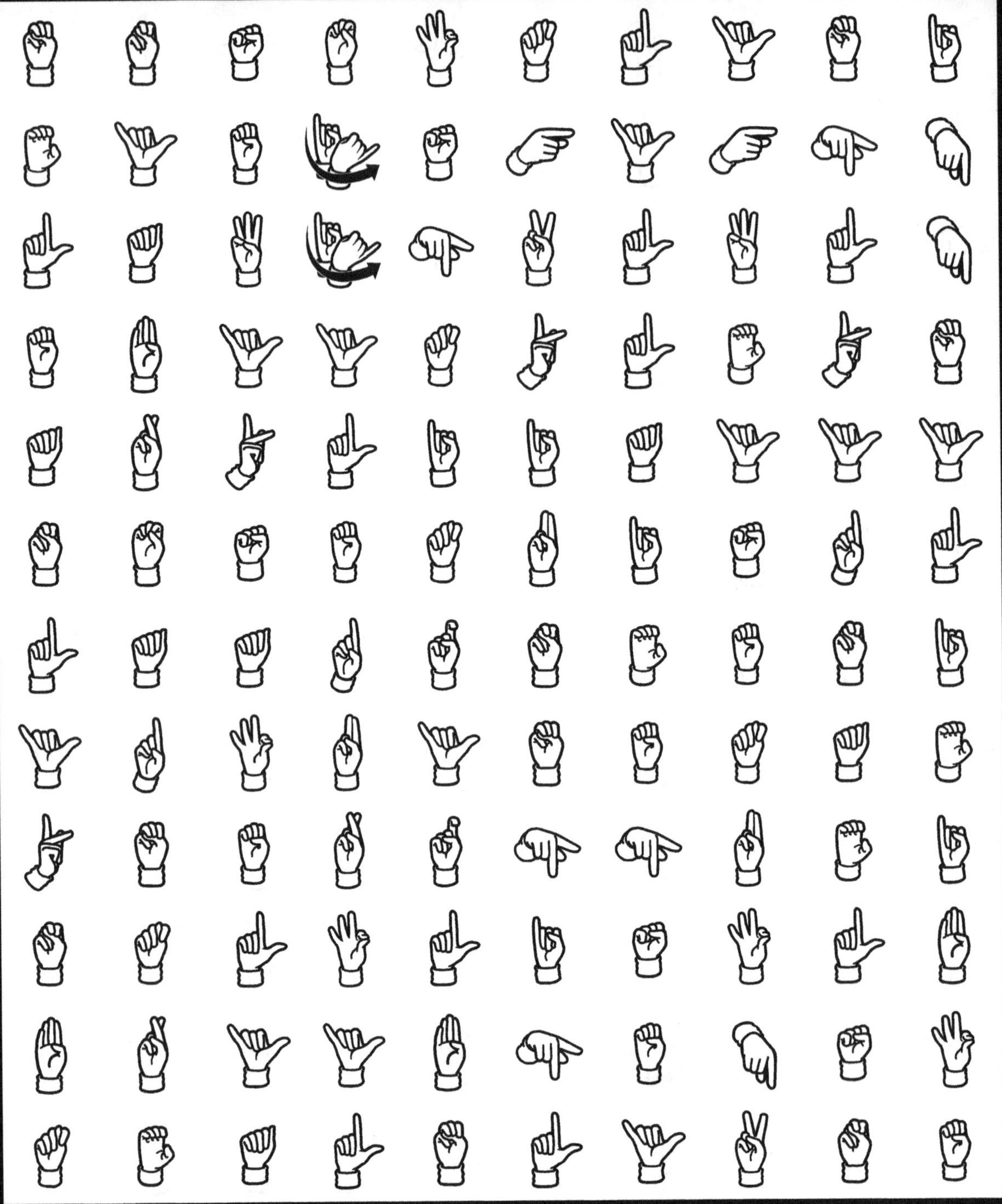

ABROAD	FLUENTLY
CALMLY	ICILY
CLEANLY	RUDELY
DEEPLY	SAFELY
ESPECIALLY	SOFTLY

34 ADVERBS MIX 3

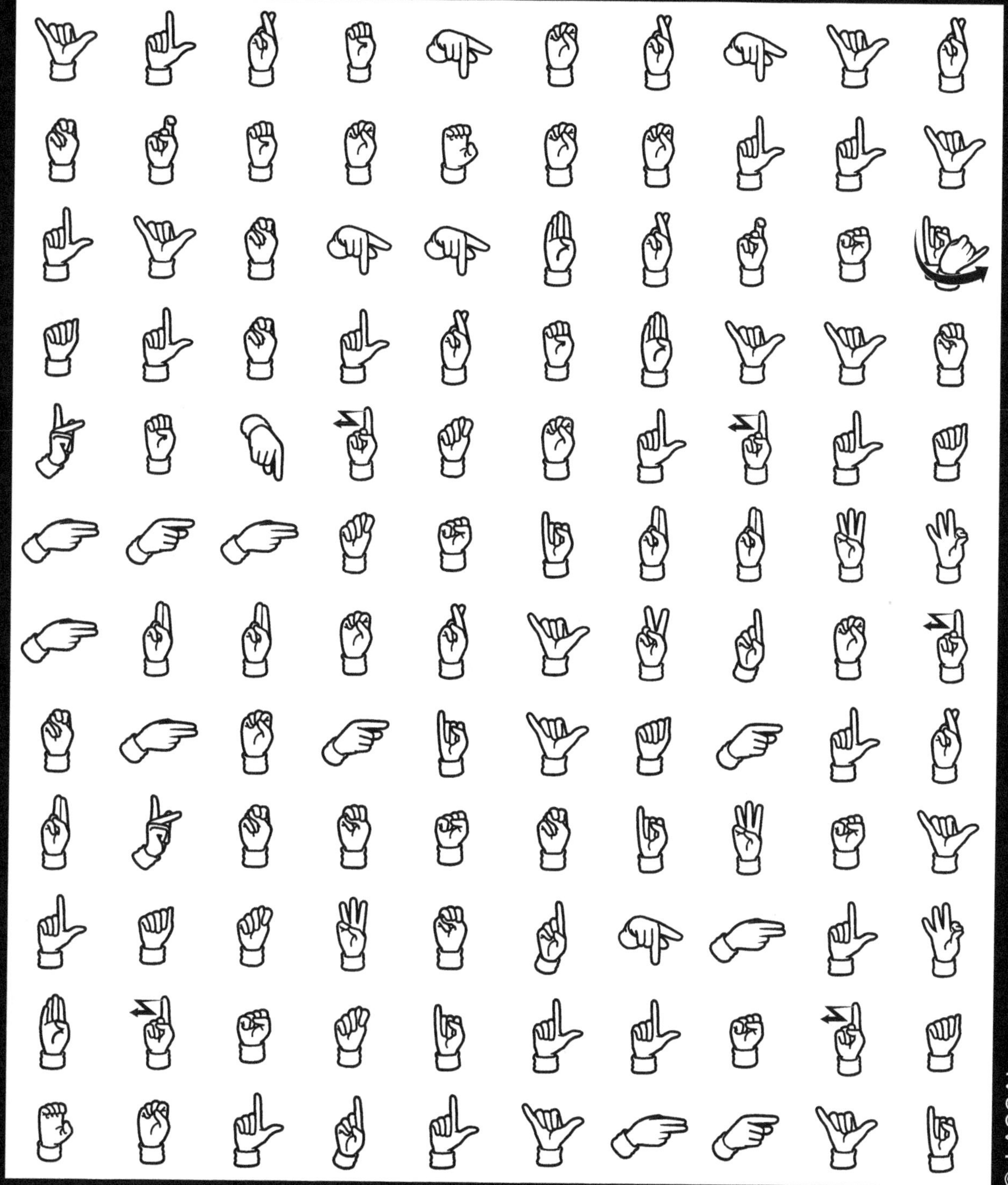

ALWAYS
ANGRILY
COLDLY
COOLLY
HUGELY

PROPERLY
PROUDLY
SLOWLY
STILL
UTTERLY

35 ADVERBS MIX 4

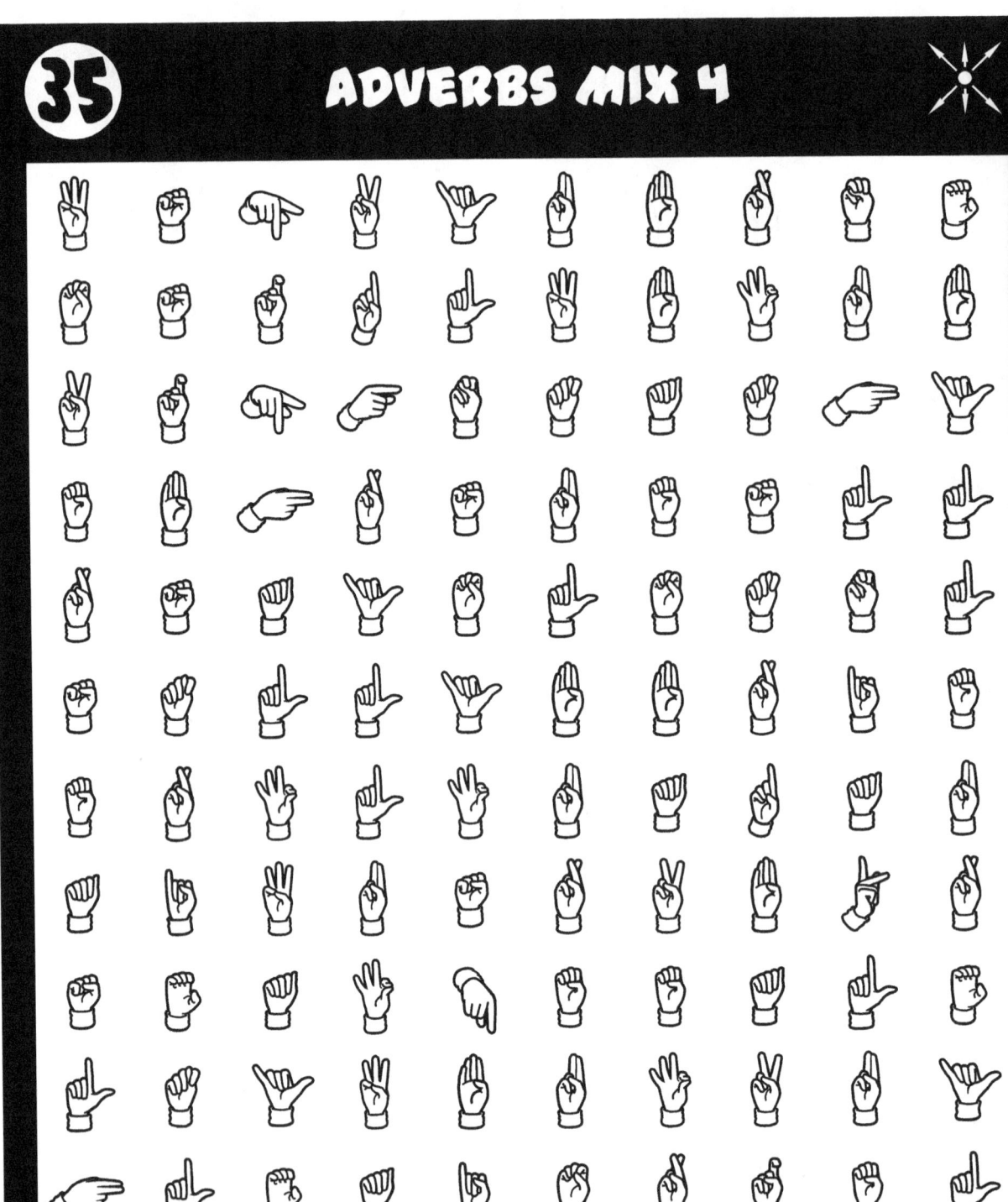

AROUND
AWFULLY
CRUELLY
CUTELY
HALFWAY

NEVER
OVERSEAS
PROBABLY
STRICTLY
SUBTLY

36 ADVERBS MIX 5

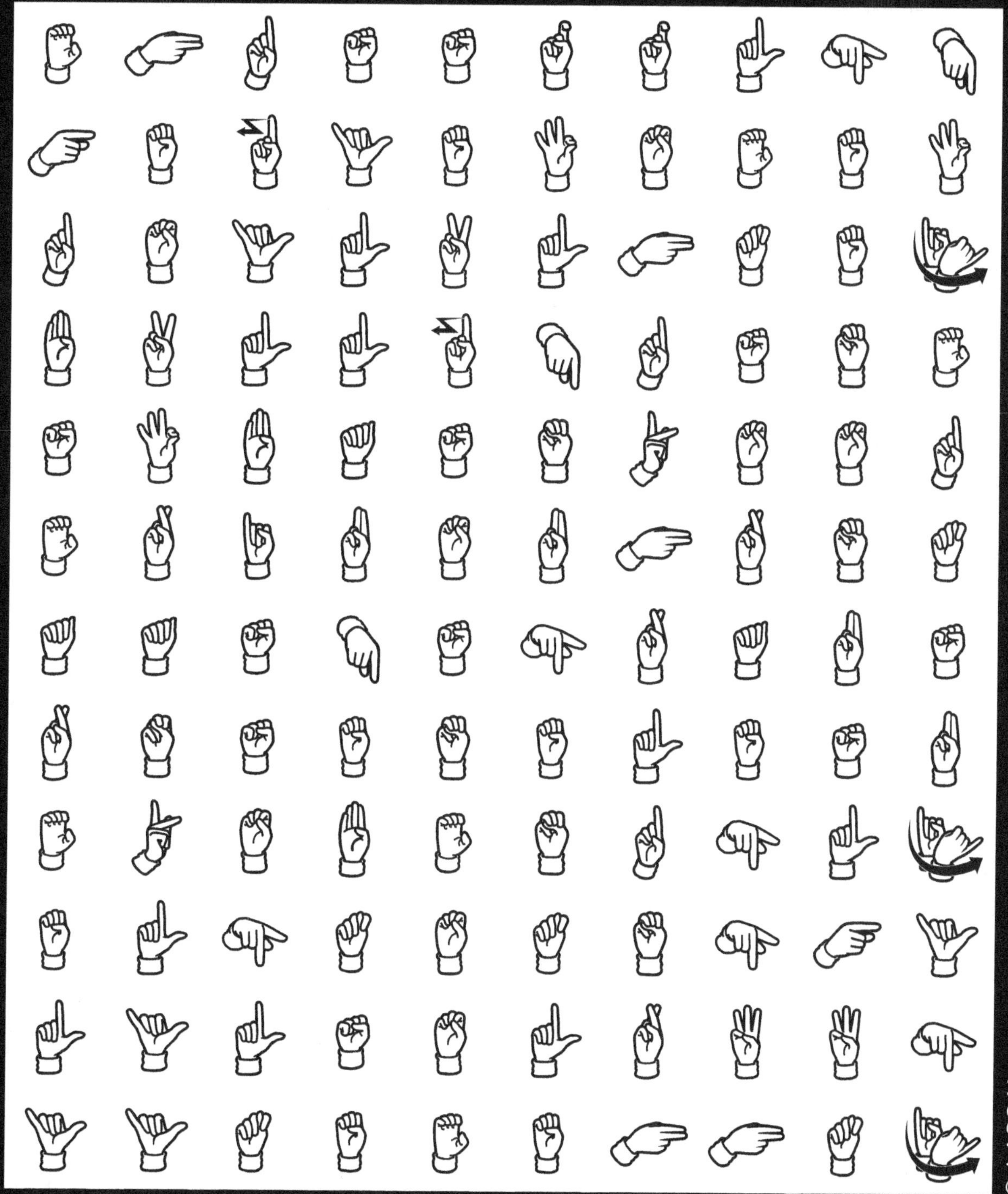

ALMOST
CORRECTLY
EQUALLY

FRANKLY
JUST
POSSIBLY

SCARCELY
SELDOM
SURELY

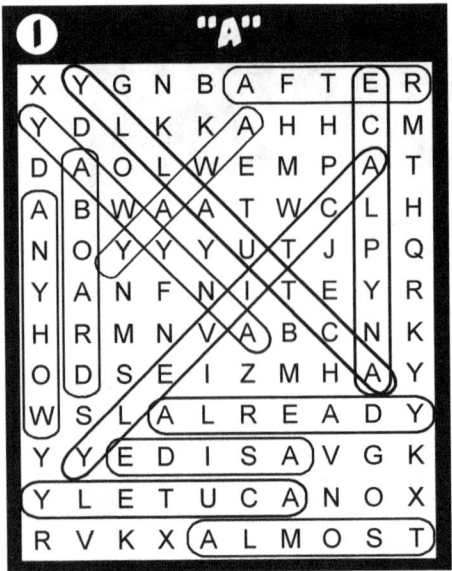
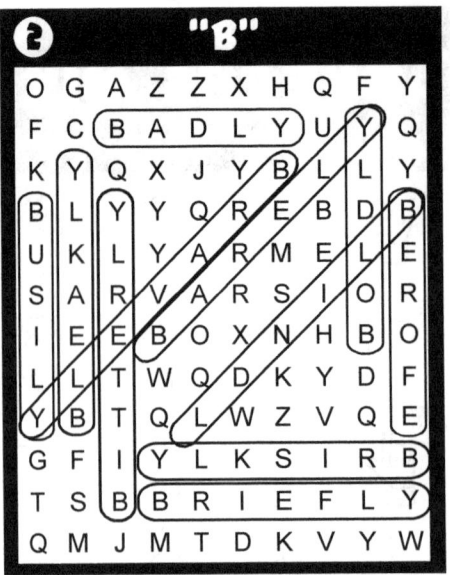

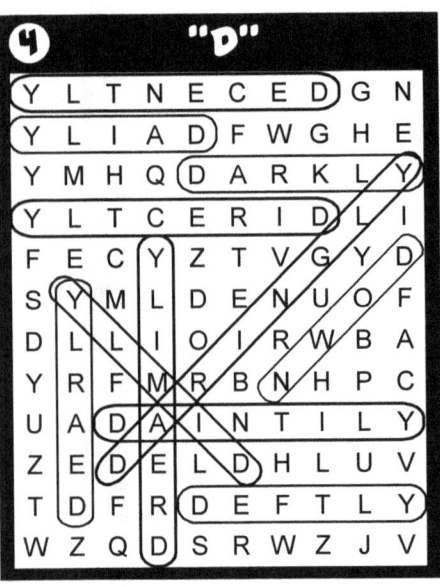

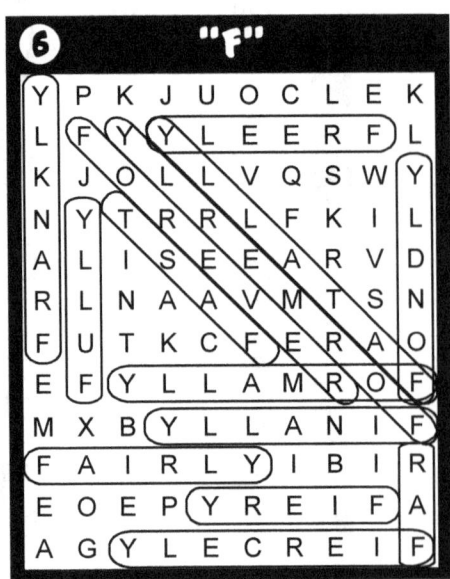
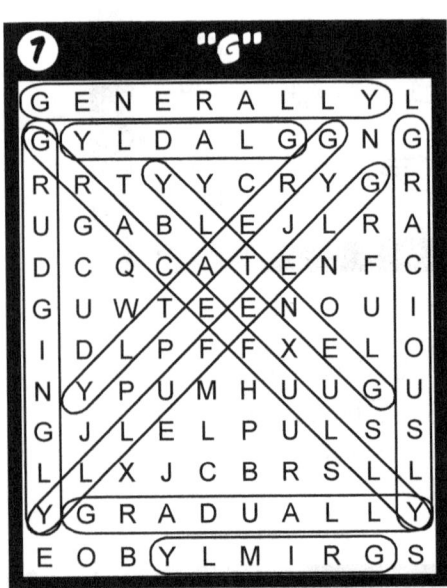
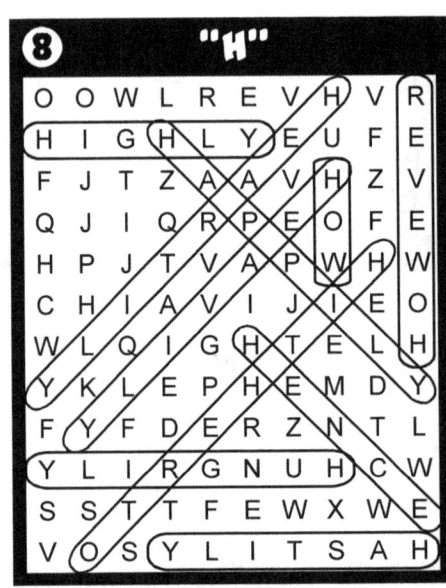
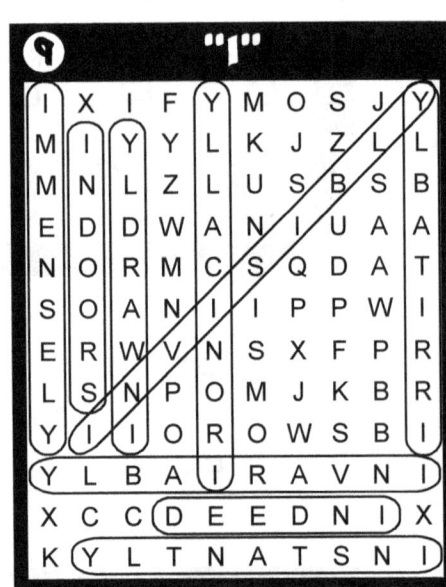

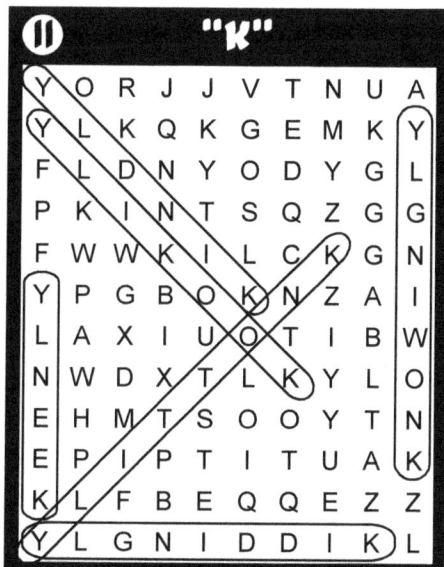

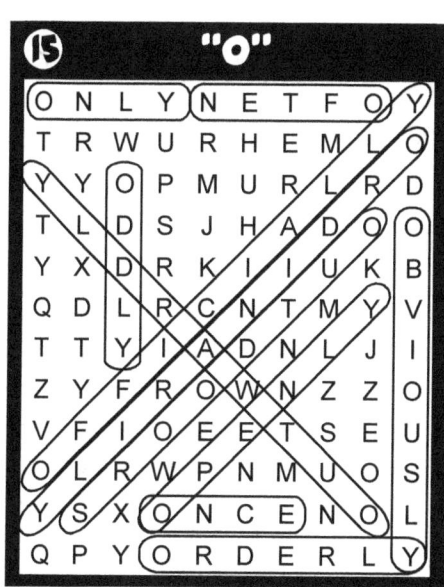
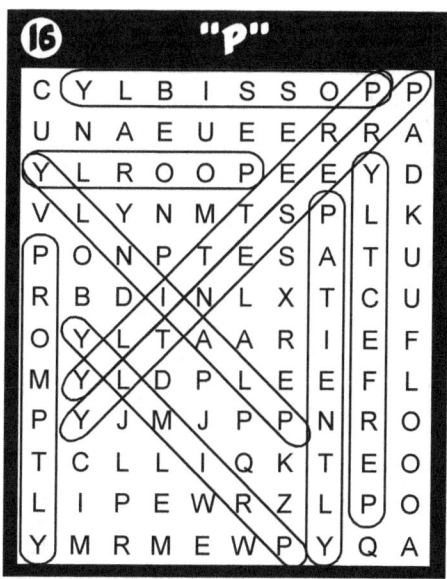
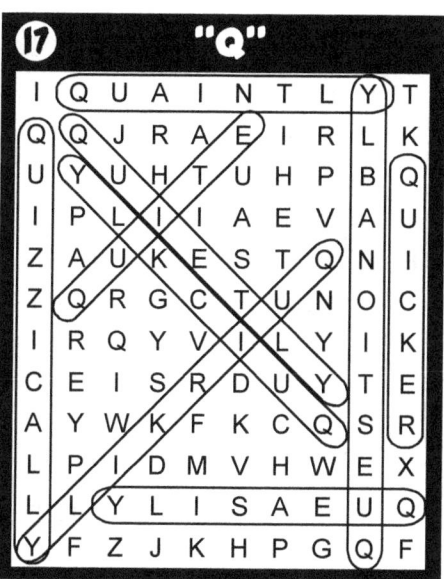
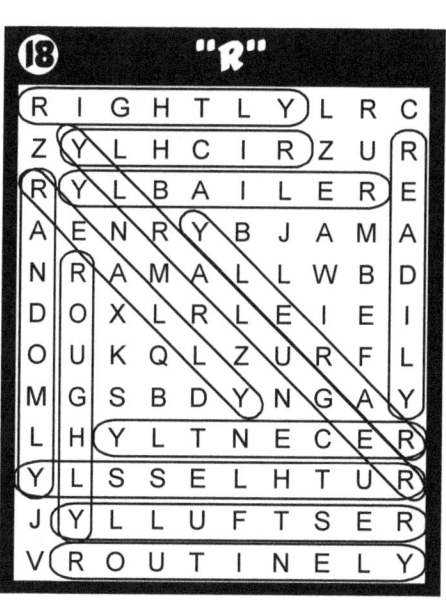

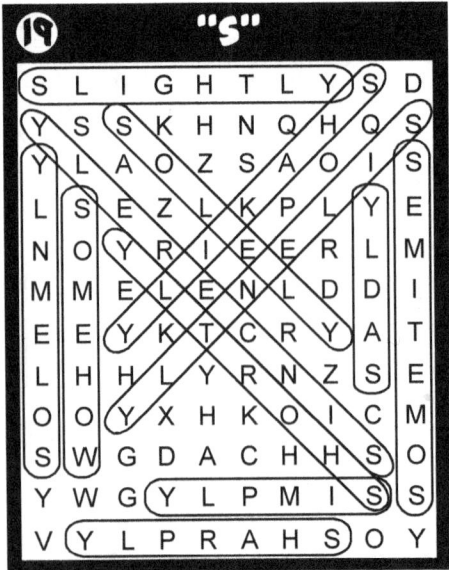
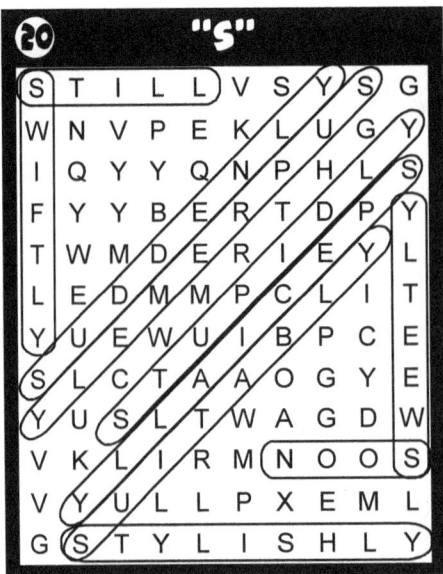
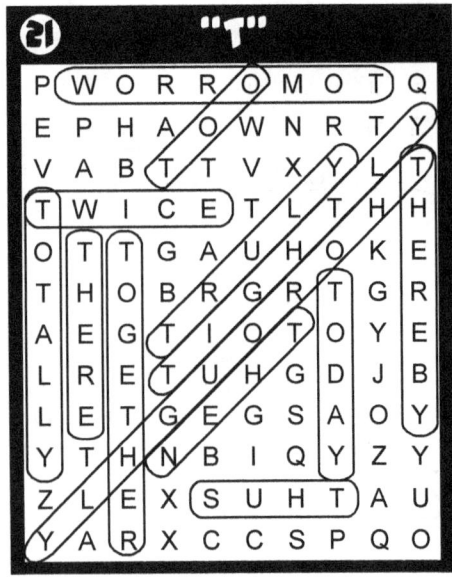
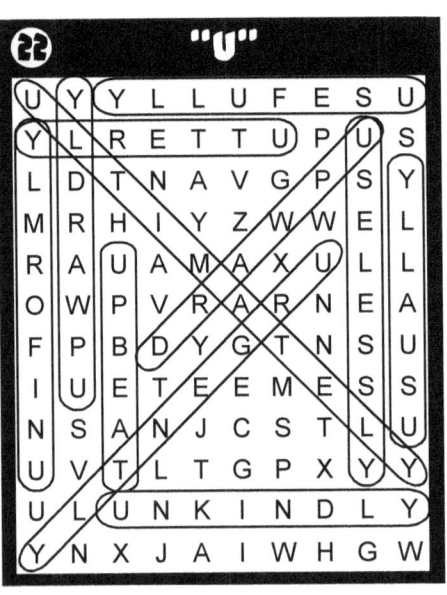
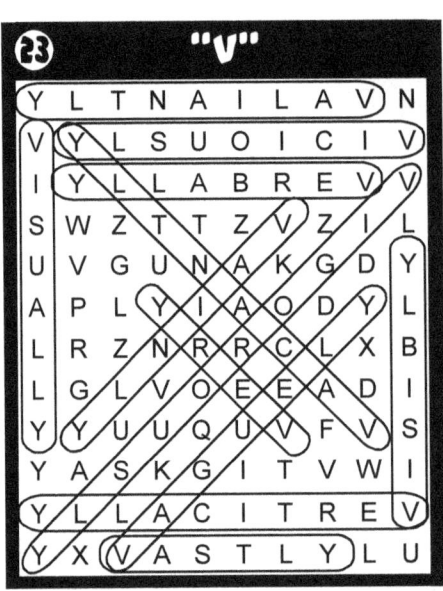

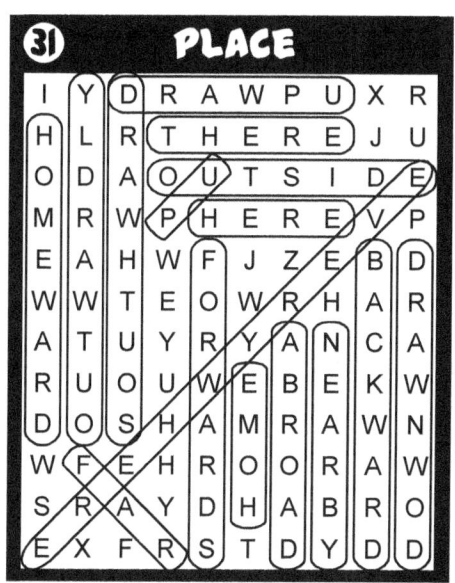
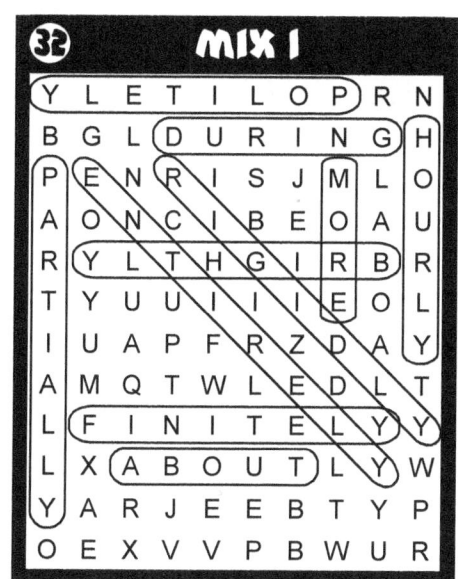
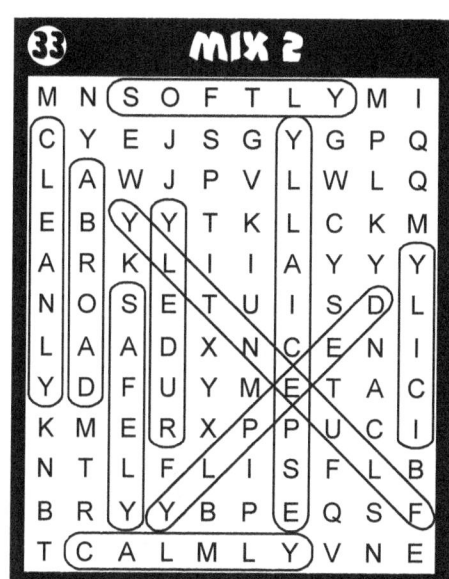
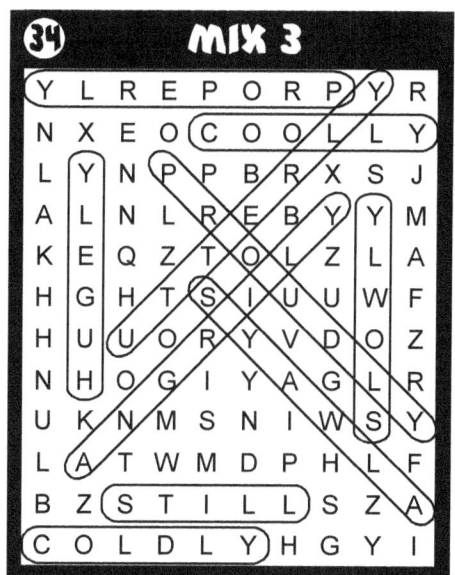
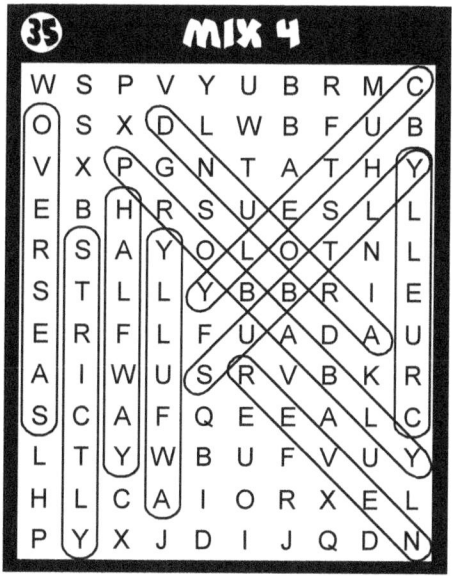
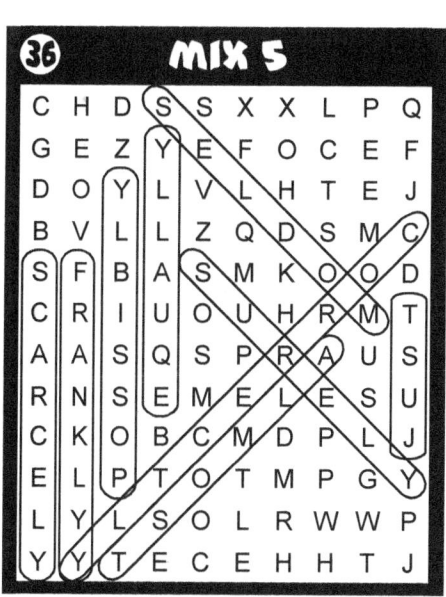

FINGER ALPHABET COOL KIDS
36 WORD SEARCH PUZZLES
WITH THE
AMERICAN **SIGN** LANGUAGE ALPHABET

 NEW

HAVE FUN & LEARN
ADJECTIVES
3RD - 5TH GRADE

ISBN 978-3-86469-104-1

SOON AVAILABLE FOR
COOL ADULTS

FINGER ALPHABET COOL KIDS
WORD SEARCH PUZZLES 36

 NEW

WITH THE
AMERICAN **SIGN** LANGUAGE ALPHABET

HAVE FUN & LEARN
ADVERBS
3RD - 5TH GRADE

ISBN 978-3-86469-108-9

SOON AVAILABLE FOR
COOL ADULTS

FINGER ALPHABET COOL KIDS
36 WORD SEARCH PUZZLES

WITH THE AMERICAN **SIGN** LANGUAGE ALPHABET

NEW

HAVE FUN & LEARN
VERBS
3RD - 5TH GRADE

ISBN 978-3-86469-106-5

SOON AVAILABLE FOR **COOL ADULTS**

HAVE FUN & LEARN!

MORE INFORMATION ABOUT UPCOMING WORD SEARCH BOOKS ON
WWW.LEGENDARYMEDIA.DE/WORDSEARCH

WANT MORE?

REVISED & APPROVED ALPHABET

DOWNLOAD FREE POSTERS WITH THE
AMERICAN SIGN LANGUAGE ALPHABET
AT

WWW.FINGERALPHABET.ORG/NORTH-AMERICA/USA
AND CHECK OUT OTHER SIGN LANGUAGE ALPHABETS

www.ingramcontent.com/pod-product-compliance
Lightning Source LLC
Chambersburg PA
CBHW081023040426
42444CB00014B/3334